AMERICA ★ THE ★ BEAUTIFUL

How to Use This Book

Look for these special features in this book:

SIDEBARS, **CHARTS**, **GRAPHS**, and original **MAPS** expand your understanding of what's being discussed—and also make useful sources for classroom reports.

FAQs answer common **F**requently **A**sked **Q**uestions about people, places, and things.

WOW FACTORS offer "Who knew?" facts to keep you thinking.

TRAVEL GUIDE gives you tips on exploring the state—either in person or right from your chair!

PROJECT ROOM provides fun ideas for school assignments and incredible research projects. Plus, there's a guide to primary sources—what they are and how to cite them.

Please note: All statistics are as up-to-date as possible at the time of publication.
Population data is taken from the 2010 census.

Consultants: William Loren Katz; D. K. Moore, Chairman, Department of Geology,
Brigham Young University–Idaho; Adam M. Sowards, Assistant Professor of History and
Environmental Science, University of Idaho; Todd Shallat, Professor of History and Director
of the Center for Idaho History and Politics, Boise State University

Book production by The Design Lab

Library of Congress Cataloging-in-Publication Data
Kent, Deborah.
 Idaho / by Deborah Kent. — Revised edition.
 pages cm. — (America the beautiful, third series)
 Includes bibliographical references and index.
 Audience: Ages 9–12.
 ISBN 978-0-531-28278-6 (lib. bdg. : alk. paper)
 1. Idaho—Juvenile literature. I. Title.
 F746.3.K455 2014
 979.6—dc23   2013044327

1 2 3 4 5 6 7 8 9 10 R 24 23 22 21 20 19 18 17 16 15

AMERICA ★ THE ★ BEAUTIFUL

Idaho

BY DEBORAH KENT

Third Series, Revised Edition

Children's Press®
An Imprint of Scholastic Inc.
New York ★ Toronto ★ London ★ Auckland ★ Sydney
Mexico City ★ New Delhi ★ Hong Kong
Danbury, Connecticut

CONTENTS

PROJECT ROOM

★

★

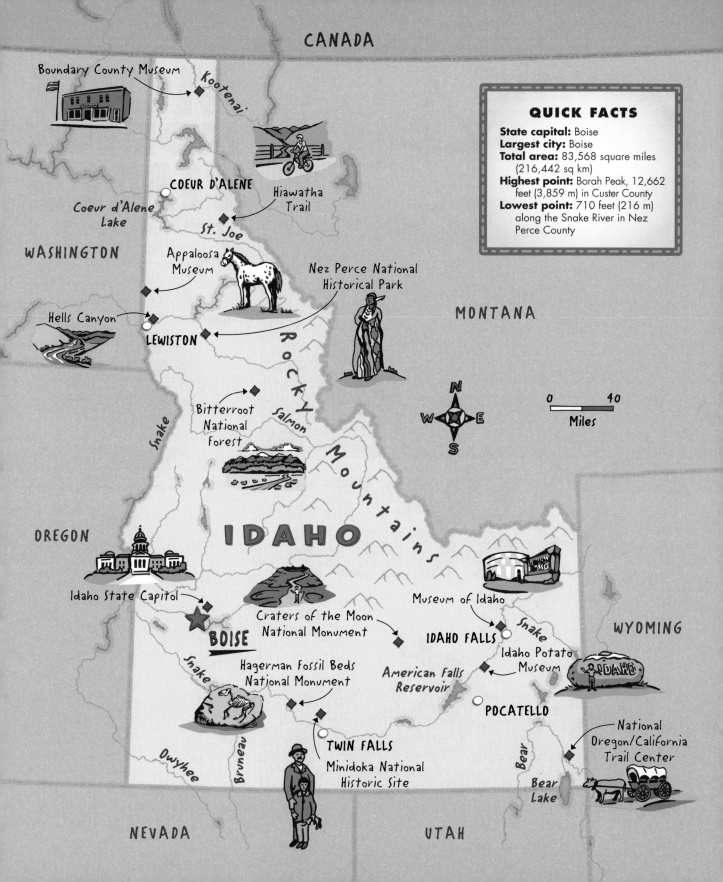

CANADA

Boundary County Museum

Kootenai

COEUR D'ALENE

Hiawatha Trail

Coeur d'Alene Lake

St. Joe

WASHINGTON

Appaloosa Museum

Nez Perce National Historical Park

MONTANA

Hells Canyon

LEWISTON

ROCKY

Salmon

Bitterroot National Forest

Mountains

OREGON

IDAHO

Museum of Idaho

Idaho State Capitol

Craters of the Moon National Monument

IDAHO FALLS

Snake

WYOMING

BOISE

Idaho Potato Museum

Hagerman Fossil Beds National Monument

Snake

American Falls Reservoir

POCATELLO

National Oregon/California Trail Center

Owyhee

Bruneau

TWIN FALLS

Minidoka National Historic Site

Bear

Bear Lake

NEVADA

UTAH

N
W E
S

0   40
Miles

Welcome to Idaho!

HOW DID IDAHO GET ITS NAME?

In 1860, the U.S. government was dividing the vast lands in the West into areas called territories. George M. Willing of Denver urged Congress to give the name "Idaho" to the land that eventually became Colorado. He claimed the name meant "gem of the mountains" in a Native American language. But when people in Colorado found out that "Idaho" was not really an Indian word, they decided to stick with "Colorado."

The word "Idaho" still floated around the West. After gold was discovered in what is now north-central Idaho, thousands of miners flooded into the region. Soon, people started working to make the area an official U.S. territory. A territory needed a name, and an old familiar word was mentioned as a possibility. In 1863, the U.S. government named this new territory "Idaho."

READ ABOUT

A winter view
of Alice Lake

CHAPTER ONE

LAND

★

WHEN PEOPLE DESCRIBE THE SCENERY OF IDAHO, THEY SOMETIMES RUN OUT OF ADJECTIVES. It is a land of starkly beautiful high deserts, spectacular waterfalls, crystal clear lakes, and breathtaking mountains. Borah Peak, the highest mountain in the state, towers 12,662 feet (3,859 meters) above sea level and is crowned with snow during most of the year. The state's lowest point is 710 feet (216 m), along the rushing Snake River. Throughout its 83,568 square miles (216,442 square kilometers), Idaho is full of surprises.

Shoshone Falls Park on the Snake River

Idaho Geo-Facts

Along with the state's geographical highlights, this chart ranks Idaho's land, water, and total area compared to all other states.

Total area; rank	83,568 square miles (216,442 sq km); 14th
Land; rank	82,643 square miles (214,045 sq km); 11th
Water; rank	926 square miles (2,398 sq km); 33rd
Inland water; rank	926 square miles (2,398 sq km); 25th
Geographic center	Custer County, southwest of Challis
Latitude	42° N to 49° N
Longitude	111° W to 117° W
Highest point	Borah Peak, 12,662 feet (3,859 m) in Custer County
Lowest point	710 feet (216 m) along the Snake River in Nez Perce County
Largest city	Boise
Longest river	Snake River

Source: U.S. Census Bureau, 2010 census

The tiny state of Rhode Island could fit into Idaho 54 times! Idaho could fit into Alaska, the biggest state, seven times!

GETTING TO KNOW IDAHO

Idaho lies in the northwestern region of the United States. It is roughly rectangular in shape, with a long, narrow extension called the Panhandle stretching north between Washington to the west and Montana to the east. The Snake River forms much of Idaho's border with Oregon, its other western neighbor. To the

Idaho Topography

Use the color-coded elevation chart to see on the map Idaho's high points (dark red) and low points (green). Elevation is measured as the distance above or below sea level.

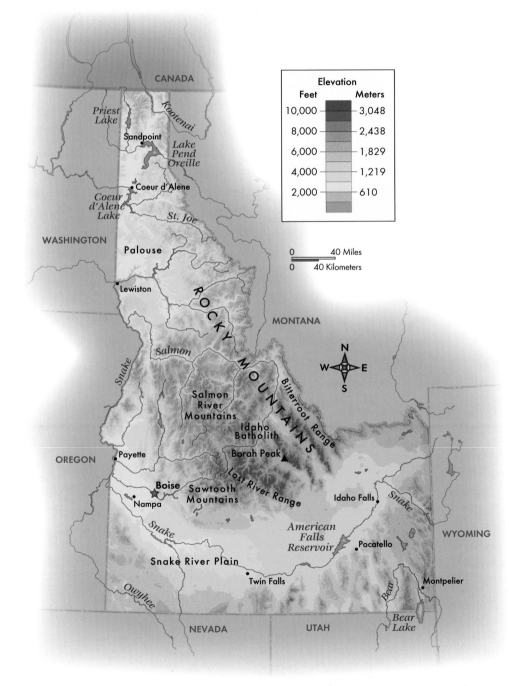

Elevation	
Feet	Meters
10,000	3,048
8,000	2,438
6,000	1,829
4,000	1,219
2,000	610

south lie Utah and Nevada, and Wyoming is to the southeast. The northern edge of the Panhandle borders the Canadian province of British Columbia.

SHAPING THE LAND

Idaho's plains and mountains look rock solid, but in fact they are always shifting. The land we call Idaho was formed by a series of earthquakes, volcanic eruptions, and slow shifts of the **tectonic** plates that make up the earth's outer layer. Idaho in its present form was created over millions of years.

About 250 million years ago, central Idaho lay at the western shore of a continent. Slowly, yet with tremendous force, a vast tectonic plate nudged its way beneath the continent's edge. At the same time, the plate forming the continent moved westward. As the plates slid over one another, the upper one heaved and cracked. The fractured earth formed a series of mountains, valleys, and canyons. At one time, many of Idaho's mountains were twice as high as they are now. Huge chunks broke off and tumbled eastward into present-day Montana.

Idaho's tectonic plate once rested atop an intense hot spot, a place where molten rock and gases bubble close to the earth's surface. As the plate inched its way across this hot spot, melted rock, or magma, seeped up through cracks in the earth's crust. The plains of southern Idaho were formed as this melted rock cooled and hardened. Here and there, the seeping magma formed rounded mounds, or buttes. In other places, oozing lava sculpted strange towers, tubes, and pyramids.

Idaho's landscape is constantly changing. Most changes take longer than a human lifetime. Others happen overnight, as when earthquakes occur. The 1983 Borah Peak earthquake shattered the ground in spectac-

WORD TO KNOW

tectonic *describing the structure of the earth's outer layer*

SEE IT HERE!

HAGERMAN FOSSIL BEDS

The Hagerman Fossil Beds in southern Idaho have yielded the bones of saber-toothed cats, giant ground sloths, mastodons, ancient horses, and more than 200 other animals and plants. Scientists uncover about 3,000 fossil fragments each year. You can watch scientists at work as they unearth and preserve long-buried bones. Check out the plaster cast of a fossilized horse and a mural showing how the valley may have looked when ancient horses roamed.

Idahoans assess the damage following the Borah Peak earthquake of October 1983.

ular ways, changed the flow of rivers and streams, and caused landslides.

LAND REGIONS

Idaho has three land regions. The northernmost is the Palouse. The Idaho Batholith is the mountainous region

WATER BENEATH THE GROUND

Beneath the high desert of southern Idaho lies a vast treasure—a huge underground reservoir called the Snake River Plain **Aquifer**. Water from melting snow seeps into the earth and is stored in **porous** basalt rock, which soaks it up like a sponge. Scientists estimate that the aquifer contains as much water as Lake Erie, one of the Great Lakes!

WOW

The Island Park Caldera near Ashton is the gigantic crater of a volcano that collapsed millions of years ago. Hundreds of square miles of land lie within the caldera. Fallout from the volcano's collapse has been found as far away as Kansas.

WORDS TO KNOW

aquifer *an underground layer of soil or loose rock that holds water*

porous *capable of absorbing liquids*

A horse grazing near the Sawtooth Mountains

in the center of the state. (A batholith is a large body of underground rock formed from cooled liquid magma deep in the earth's crust.) The Snake River Plain lies in Idaho's southern region.

The Palouse

The Palouse is an area of rolling hills that covers roughly 4,000 square miles (10,000 sq km). It stretches from north of Lewiston to the southern end of Coeur d'Alene Lake, and across the state line to Washington. The mild winters, wet springs, and dry summers provide ideal conditions for growing certain varieties of wheat. Just north of the Palouse, in the northernmost tip of Idaho, lie the Selkirk Mountains.

Q: HOW MANY PEAKS IN IDAHO ARE MORE THAN 12,000 FEET (3,658 M) TALL?

A: Idaho has nine "twelvers," mountains that are 12,000 feet (3,658 m) or more in height.

The Idaho Batholith

The Idaho Batholith includes several mountain ranges that are part of the sprawling Rocky Mountains, a wide band of rugged ranges that run the length of the state and from Canada to Mexico. Major ranges include the Bitterroot Range, the Lost River Range, the Salmon River Mountains, the Coeur d'Alene Mountains, and the Sawtooth Mountains. Rivers that flow through the Idaho Batholith include the Payette, Selway, Salmon, Lochsa, Clearwater, and Boise. Large amounts of snow fall throughout the region, and temperatures are generally cool, averaging between 35 and 50 degrees Fahrenheit (1.7 and 10 degrees Celsius) throughout the year.

Lake Pend Oreille, the biggest lake in Idaho, is 65 miles (105 km) long and 1,150 feet (351 m) deep in some places.

White-water rafters in Tappan Falls in the Middle Fork of the Salmon River

Hells Canyon of the Snake River, which lies on the border between Idaho and Oregon, is the deepest river gorge in North America—even deeper than the Grand Canyon of Arizona. On the Idaho side, it plunges 7,900 feet (2,408 m) from the highest peak to the canyon floor.

WORD TO KNOW

precipitation *all water that falls to the earth, including rain, sleet, hail, snow, dew, fog, or mist*

The Snake River Plain

The Snake River Plain stretches westward about 400 miles (640 km) from northwestern Idaho to the Idaho-Oregon border. The region is relatively flat and in the 19th century provided an ideal surface for wagon trains heading farther west. Many of Idaho's largest cities, such as Boise, Nampa, and Idaho Falls, lie in the Snake River Plain. The region is a major agricultural region, where sugar beets, potatoes, grains, and vegetables are grown. Livestock grazing and dairy farms are found in many areas of the plain.

CLIMATE

In general, the higher the altitude in Idaho, the cooler the climate. The mildest climate is found in the state's lowest regions, especially along the Clearwater and Salmon rivers, and in parts of the Snake River Valley. Moist Pacific winds bring rain and snow to northern Idaho, whereas the south tends to be much drier. Some valleys in the southwest re-ceive only 10 inches (25 centimeters) of **precipitation** a year.

Idaho sometimes experiences scorching summer days, especially in the southern part of the state. It is not uncommon for the temperature to soar higher than 100°F (38°C). But Idaho seldom experiences extreme summer heat for more than a week at a time. In the same way, winter temperatures can plummet to −20°F (−29°C) or lower, but periods of extreme cold are usually over within a few days.

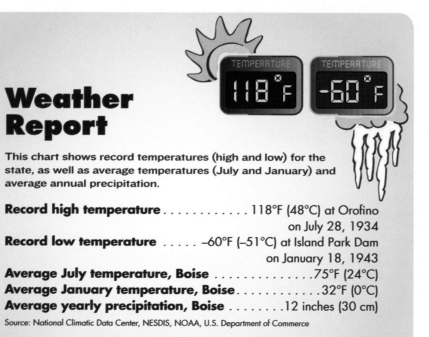

Weather Report

This chart shows record temperatures (high and low) for the state, as well as average temperatures (July and January) and average annual precipitation.

Record high temperature . . . . 118°F (48°C) at Orofino on July 28, 1934

Record low temperature . . . . . −60°F (−51°C) at Island Park Dam on January 18, 1943

Average July temperature, Boise . . . . .75°F (24°C)

Average January temperature, Boise . . . . .32°F (0°C)

Average yearly precipitation, Boise . . . . .12 inches (30 cm)

Source: National Climatic Data Center, NESDIS, NOAA, U.S. Department of Commerce

Idahoans enjoy the snow by engaging in cross-country skiing and other activities.

Snowfall can be heavy in the mountains. On February 20, 1954, Mullan Pass had a record 15 feet (4.6 m) of snow!

PLANT LIFE

About 40 percent of Idaho's land is covered with evergreen forests. Among the most common trees in northern Idaho are the western white pine, white fir, and Douglas fir. Douglas fir is also found in the forested areas of the south, along with lodgepole pine and ponderosa pine. Some deciduous trees (trees that lose their leaves in autumn) grow on the lower slopes of the mountains. These include aspen, maple, birch, and mountain ash. Stands of cottonwood grow along the banks of rivers and streams.

Idaho has 9,322,000 acres (3,772,000 hectares) of roadless wilderness, more than any other state except Alaska!

A stand of sagebrush and gray rabbitbrush in Bruneau Dunes State Park

Idaho's grasslands are fields of wheatgrass, fescue, and the white-flowered shrub syringa, which is Idaho's state flower. In the driest regions grow tangles of sagebrush, rabbitbrush, and greasewood.

ANIMAL LIFE

The remote mountains and canyons of Idaho are among the last refuges of some of North America's rarest birds and animals. Grizzly bears, gray wolves, bison, and whooping cranes cling to survival in the state. Black bears, coyotes, and bobcats have healthy populations. Mountain goats and bighorn sheep live among the high peaks, and mule deer and pronghorn browse at lower levels. Jackrabbits bound over the grasslands

AN UNWELCOME INVADER

A tough, dense grass called downy brome or cheatgrass, which originally came from southern Europe, crowds out many of Idaho's native grasses. Cheatgrass offers little nourishment to grazing animals. And its leaves die by midsummer, leaving plenty of dry fuel to feed wildfires.

MINI-BIO

DARWIN K. VEST: A PASSION FOR SPIDERS

For much of his life, Darwin K. Vest (1951–1999) ran the projector at a movie theater in Moscow, Idaho. Yet his true passion was not for movies but for spiders. Although Vest had no formal education as a scientist, he became a world expert on spiders and their venom. He identified and studied the hobo spider, a poisonous spider that came to the Northwest from Europe sometime in the 1960s.

? **Want to know more?** Visit www.factsfornow .scholastic.com and enter the keyword **Idaho**.

FAQ

Q8 DO ANY POISONOUS CREATURES LIVE IN IDAHO?

A8 Idaho has many kinds of snakes, but only one, the western rattlesnake, is poisonous. One spider species found in Idaho, the hobo spider, has a poisonous bite.

in the south. Even the desert harbors a variety of creatures, including the horned toad and whip-tailed lizard.

Every year, thousands of salmon fight their way upstream to lay eggs in the Snake, Salmon, and other Idaho rivers. After they hatch, the young salmon make their way downstream, all the way to the Pacific Ocean.

Sockeye salmon

SPECIES AT RISK

The U.S. Bureau of Land Management has classified five plant species in Idaho as threatened. They are MacFarlane's four o'clock, Spalding's silene, slick spot peppergrass, Ute ladies' tresses, and water howellia. A threatened species is one that is likely to become endangered.

Several animal species in Idaho are also classified as threatened or endangered. Among them are the sockeye salmon, woodland caribou, grizzly bear, lynx, and northern Idaho ground squirrel.

THINK ABOUT IT!

Bringing Back Grizzly Bears

Grizzly bears once roamed Idaho's Bitterroot Range, but none have been seen there since the 1940s. For years, environmentalists and local Idahoans have debated returning grizzlies to the area. Environmentalists argue that a protected habitat should be set aside for the bears. Many people in the area object, fearing that grizzlies will leave the preserve to attack humans and livestock. For the time being, the Idaho Fish and Game Commission (IFGC) has stepped into the debate and is having the last word. In a statement issued in May 2013, the IFGC firmly stated, "The Commission and the State of Idaho have repeatedly opposed introductions of grizzly bears in the Bitterroot area."

MINI-BIO

CECIL D. ANDRUS: SPEAKING OUT FOR THE ENVIRONMENT

Cecil Andrus (1931–) grew up in Oregon logging towns. In 1955, he moved to Orofino, Idaho, to work in the timber industry. He wanted to protect Idaho's land from overdevelopment. In 1960, he won a seat in the state senate, and he was elected governor in 1970. He eventually served 14 years as governor (1971–1977 and 1987–1995), during which time he worked to preserve forestland and clean up polluted lakes and rivers. He also fought to keep the federal government from storing nuclear waste in Idaho and worked to protect endangered salmon in the Snake River.

? **Want to know more?** Visit www.factsfornow .scholastic.com and enter the keyword **Idaho**.

CARING FOR THE LAND

As long as humans have lived on the land called Idaho, they have been sustained by its rich natural resources. Plants and animals provided food for Native people and later for European pioneers. Beavers and other fur-bearing animals provided income to trappers and traders, and forests gave rise to a booming timber industry. Streams and wells irrigated farmers' fields.

Today, most Idahoans recognize that human activity has had a serious impact on the state's environment. The water level in the Snake River Plain Aquifer has declined by about 15 percent since the 1950s because it's been used to water land. Logging has damaged the habitat of many plants and animals. Large creatures such as the wolf, cougar, and grizzly need extensive tracts of land on which to hunt. Logging cuts these large territories into small, unconnected patches.

Idaho National Park Areas

This map shows some of Idaho's national parks, monuments, preserves, and other areas protected by the National Park Service.

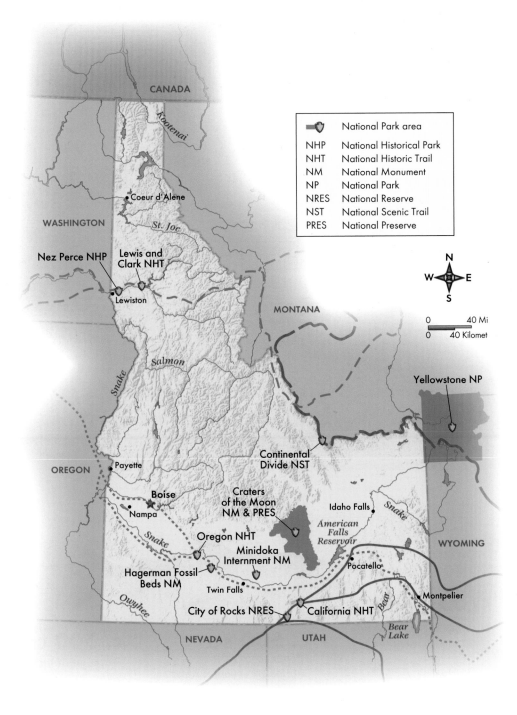

National Park area
NHP — National Historical Park
NHT — National Historic Trail
NM — National Monument
NP — National Park
NRES — National Reserve
NST — National Scenic Trail
PRES — National Preserve

CANADA

Kootenai

• Coeur d'Alene

WASHINGTON

St. Joe

Nez Perce NHP

Lewis and Clark NHT

• Lewiston

MONTANA

Snake

Salmon

N
W · E
S

0 — 40 Mi
0 — 40 Kilomet

Yellowstone NP

OREGON

• Payette

Continental Divide NST

Boise

• Nampa

Craters of the Moon NM & PRES

Idaho Falls

Snake

American Falls Reservoir

WYOMING

Snake

Oregon NHT

Minidoka Internment NM

Hagerman Fossil Beds NM

• Twin Falls

• Pocatello

Bear

• Montpelier

City of Rocks NRES

California NHT

Owyhee

Bear Lake

NEVADA

UTAH

22

Early hunters
pursued mammoth
and other big game.

c. 5500 BCE

*Hunters begin throwing
spears using the atlatl*

▲ **c. 500 BCE**

*People begin drying
salmon on wooden racks*

c. 500 CE

*People in Idaho begin
using bows and arrows*

CHAPTER TWO

FIRST PEOPLE

★

MOST EXPERTS AGREE THAT THE FIRST HUMANS IN WHAT IS NOW IDAHO ARRIVED ABOUT 15,000 YEARS AGO. Idaho's earliest people were hunters. In fact, evidence found in Wilson Butte Cave in southern Idaho shows that they hunted giant bison. The newcomers to Idaho also hunted mammoth, caribou, and musk ox. At the time, the climate in the region was cold and harsh.

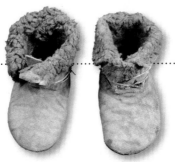

c. 1300 ►
Shoshonean people migrate into Idaho from the south

Shoshone moccasins

c. 1700
Shoshones and Nez Perce obtain horses

EARLY PEOPLE

As the centuries passed, the climate grew warmer and the ice began to melt away. Trees and grasses flourished, and game became more plentiful. By about 5500 BCE, people in Idaho hunted using a spear-throwing device called an atlatl. The atlatl is a long, forked stick. The hunter fitted the spear shaft into the fork and used the atlatl to hurl it forward with great force.

By about 3500 BCE, people in southern Idaho had learned to grind nuts and seeds on a flat stone. They rolled a long, rounded stone over the seeds, much as we use a rolling pin to flatten dough. People farther north chiseled a hollow into a large stone to make a bowl. They put nuts and seeds in the bowl and ground them with a smaller stone.

In northern Idaho, people waited each year for the arrival of the salmon. The vast schools of fish fighting their way upstream to lay their eggs meant food and celebration. People caught the fish in great nets weighted down with stones. When the salmon run was over, however, hungry times might set in again.

About 2,500 years ago, people discovered a way to dry salmon on wooden racks. This dried salmon could last for several months. A good supply of dried salmon insured the people against hunger, even in the coldest winter.

A major development came about 1,500 years ago. At about that time, Idaho's people, especially those living in southern Idaho, began hunting with bows and arrows. The bow and arrow was more effective than the atlatl in bringing down game. Some of the finest bows were made from the horns of bighorn sheep.

Sometime around 1300 CE, several groups of hunters and gatherers moved into southern Idaho from parts of

This painting by 19th-century German-born painter Albert Bierstadt shows a Shoshone encampment.

Nevada and Utah. The Shoshonean people, as they are called, shared similar languages and customs. They traveled in groups of extended families. They had no leaders, though respected hunters now and then organized large-scale rabbit or bison hunts.

In Idaho, the Shoshonean people fell into two main groups: Shoshones and Northern Paiutes. Shoshones hunted on most of the Snake River Plateau and north into the Bitterroot Range. Northern Paiutes lived in the arid deserts of southwestern Idaho. Panakwates were Northern Paiutes who often traveled with Shoshones.

WORD TO KNOW

breechcloth *a garment worn by a man over his lower body*

Crickets and grasshoppers, which are rich in protein, were a valuable food source for the Northern Paiute. They might have been fried to a crisp or mashed and eaten with ground seeds.

A group of Bannocks, a Native group associated with the Shoshone

SHOSHONES

By the 1700s, the Shoshone population had grown considerably in present-day Idaho. They moved from place to place in search of game or to gather certain kinds of edible seeds and roots. When they camped, they set up cone-shaped tents called tipis. To form a tipi, Shoshones leaned several poles against each other, tied them together at the top, and covered them with animal skins.

Shoshones used clay from the riverbanks to make bowls and jugs for carrying water. They made clothing from deer or rabbit skins or by weaving cloth out of plant fibers. Women wore long skirts, and men usually wore a simple **breechcloth**. In the winter, men and women draped blankets over their shoulders and wore rabbit-skin moccasins with the fur on the inside.

NORTHERN PAIUTES

Northern Paiutes lived in a desert environment. This called for strength and resourcefulness. They knew where to find springs among the bare rocks and sagebrush

Native American Peoples

(Before European Contact)

This map shows the general area of Native American peoples before European settlers arrived.

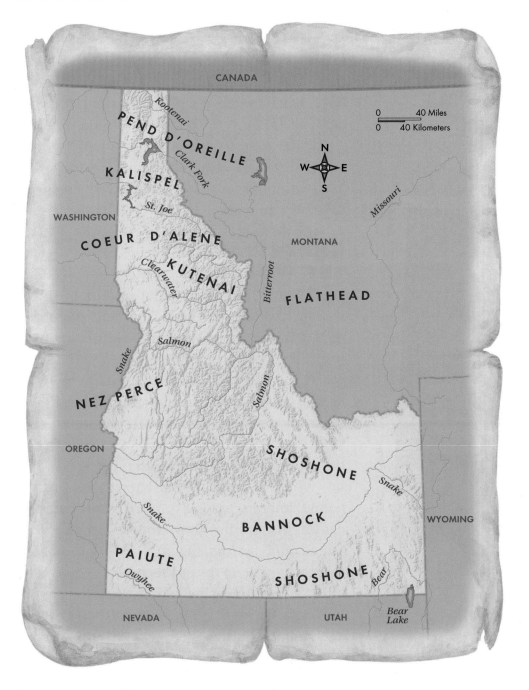

VOICE FOR THE NEZ PERCE PEOPLE

Allen Slickpoo (1929–2013) grew up on the Nez Perce reservation in northern Idaho. His grandparents taught him the history and stories of their people. When he was 10, Slickpoo moved to the town of Stites, where he enrolled in public school and learned to speak English. After a stint in the armed services, he attended the University of Idaho for two years. At the age of 22, he became the youngest member ever elected to the Nez Perce governing council. He wrote down the Nez Perce language, legends, and customs and published them in *Nu Mee Poom Tit Wah Tit: Nez Perce Legends.*

A Nez Perce baby in a cradle board, a type of infant carrier

clumps. They dug for edible roots and hunted rabbits and birds. In the summers, they feasted on pine nuts, the seeds of the piñon pine.

NORTHERN NATIONS

The largest Indian nation in northern Idaho was the Nimi'ipuu, or Nez Perce people. Nez Perce lived in the mountains and valleys of Idaho and northeastern Oregon. Kutenai and Coeur d'Alene peoples also lived in the north. Several families lived together in a house made of branches covered with woven mats.

UNDERSTANDING THE WORLD

Each Native group in Idaho had its own stories of how the earth and humans were created. They also had stories that explained the beginnings of the sun, the moon, and the stars. Native people believed that spirits lived in all of the plants and animals around them. The rocks and streams, clouds and stars were living spirits, too. The sun and moon were some of the most powerful spirits in the universe.

When the spirits were happy with human beings, there was plenty of fish and game to eat. If the spirits grew angry, food became scarce and storms raged. Native people did their best to keep the spirits happy. When they killed a deer, they thanked its spirit for providing food. They sang a song of gratitude so that deer would continue coming to the village.

This Shoshone painting illustrates a buffalo dance held after a hunt.

Most of Idaho's Native peoples saw the bear, the wolf, and the coyote as strong and important spirits. Coyote was the central character in many stories. He was a clever trickster who often brought mischief into the world.

According to the Nez Perce people, long, long ago the earth was a beautiful place filled with plants and animals of all kinds. There were no human beings. A fierce monster lived in the Clearwater Valley and began to devour all the animals it could find. Coyote got angry and killed the monster with a stone knife. He chopped up the monster's body and scattered the pieces. Each piece became a Native nation, each with its own strengths and homeland. The last drops of the monster's blood landed in the Clearwater Valley. They sprang up as the proud, strong Nez Perce Nation.

SEE IT HERE!

FORT HALL INDIAN RESERVATION

The Fort Hall Indian Reservation near Pocatello is home to Idaho's Shoshone and Bannock nations today. The Shoshone-Bannock Tribal Museum tells their story through artifacts, art, and photos. The Shoshone-Bannock Indian Festival and All-Indian Rodeo are held every August, and draw crowds from all over the United States and Canada.

FAQ ★ ★ ★

Q8 HOW DID NEZ PERCE AND SHOSHONES CHOOSE THEIR LEADERS?

A8 The tribe elected who would have the position of chief.

THUNDERING HOOFBEATS

Sometime around 1700, the first horses galloped onto Idaho's grasslands. No one knows for sure how they got there. They may have escaped from Spanish settlements in New Mexico far to the south, or they may have arrived with Indian traders. Shoshones and Nez Perce quickly acquired horses and became expert riders.

Horses revolutionized Native life. On horseback, they explored territory far from home. They adopted many customs of the Plains Indians to the east. Nez Perce and Shoshones began to wear feather headdresses and beaded moccasins like those of the Black-foot and Lakota peoples. Men and women decorated clothing with elk teeth, porcupine quills, and shells.

A family's wealth was determined by the number and swiftness of the horses it owned. Powerful chiefs emerged to lead their people on hunts or into battle with neighboring tribes.

Tragically, horses also opened the way for terrible new diseases to reach Idaho's people. When the Nez Perce visited the Blackfoot and Crow peoples of today's Montana, they found that many of them were very ill. They had caught smallpox from European traders who traveled west along the Missouri River. When the Nez Perce returned to Idaho and Oregon, they carried the smallpox virus with them. Idaho's Nez Perce had never before been exposed to smallpox and other European diseases. Some historians believe that as many as nine out of ten Nez Perce died from these diseases before any white people ever set foot in Idaho.

Every summer, Indians from many villages gathered near where the Boise River flows into the Snake. For nearly a month, they traded, danced, and competed in games. Boys wrestled and ran footraces. In one game, a man hid a stone in one of his fists. Spectators placed bets on whether the stone was clutched in his right or his left hand.

As Nez Perce and Shoshones explored the country around them, they heard stories of strange, pale-skinned people who lived to the south. They heard about knives and axes stronger than stones and sticks that cracked like thunder and hurled fire through the air. It was hard to believe that such tales were true, yet they were heard over and over again. No one could have imagined the impact that the pale strangers and their guns would have on life in the land we now call Idaho.

Picture Yourself . . .

at a Native Gathering

For the past three days, you and your family have been on the trail south, herding the horses you are bringing to trade. Now, as you come over the crest of a hill, you see smoke from campfires and hear distant voices on the wind. You hear the steady thudding of a drum and catch the aroma of meat cooking. You wonder if the Paiute band you met last year will be here again. One of the Paiute boys beat you in wrestling, but you're bigger and stronger now, and you have a better chance at winning. As soon as you see your rival, you're going to challenge him. You can't wait to reach the camp and see all the things that people have brought to trade. Maybe you can get one of those black stone knives that Paiutes bring. Your sister wants a pair of Shoshone moccasins. You nudge your horse with your heels, and it breaks into a gallop.

Young men approaching the starting point for a horse race

32

READ ABOUT

Sacagawea leading Lewis and Clark on their expedition

1805

The Corps of Discovery crosses Idaho on its way west

1809 ▶

David Thompson builds Kullyspell House, the first white settlement in Idaho, on Lake Pend Oreille

1818

The British Snake River Brigade begins trapping in Idaho

CHAPTER THREE

EXPLORATION AND SETTLEMENT

★

IN AUGUST 1805, WHITE MEN ON HORSEBACK ARRIVED AT WHAT IS NOW THE IDAHO-MONTANA BORDER. They gazed at a forbidding landscape of mountains and canyons. Among them were Captain Meriwether Lewis, John Shields, George Drouillard, and Hugh McNeal. All four belonged to a group of explorers called the Corps of Discovery. Lewis and his party were the first people of European descent to set foot in present-day Idaho.

1822

William Henry
Ashley sends
American trappers
into the Rockies

1840s ▶

Thousands of
settlers pass through Idaho
on the Oregon Trail

1846

Great Britain and the
United States sign a treaty
establishing a boundary
between British and U.S.
territory in the Northwest

Exploration of Idaho

The colored arrows on this map show the routes taken by explorers and pioneers between 1805 and 1830.

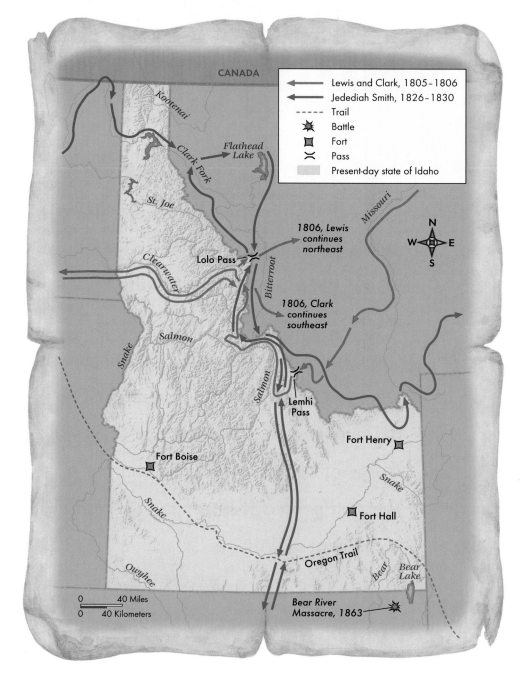

CANADA

Legend
- Lewis and Clark, 1805–1806
- Jedediah Smith, 1826–1830
- Trail
- Battle
- Fort
- Pass
- Present-day state of Idaho

Kootenai

Clark Fork

Flathead Lake

St. Joe

Missouri

1806, Lewis continues northeast

Clearwater

Lolo Pass

Bitterroot

1806, Clark continues southeast

N
W E
S

Salmon

Snake

Salmon

Lemhi Pass

Fort Henry

Fort Boise

Snake

Snake

Fort Hall

Owyhee

Oregon Trail

Bear

Bear Lake

0   40 Miles
0   40 Kilometers

Bear River Massacre, 1863

THE CORPS OF DISCOVERY

In 1803, the United States was a young nation. The colonies along the eastern seaboard had won their independence from Great Britain only 20 years before. Now many Americans were eager to go west. In 1803, the United States bought from France a vast tract of land that stretched from the Mississippi River to the Rocky Mountains. Known as the Louisiana Purchase, it nearly doubled the size of the nation.

President Thomas Jefferson organized an exploring party under Meriwether Lewis and William Clark. Lewis and Clark and the Corps of Discovery set out from St. Louis, Missouri, in 1804. Their mission was to explore the new territory and lands all the way to the Pacific Coast, including present-day Idaho.

The expedition included military men, hunters, boatmen, and an enslaved African named York. York had been Clark's companion since childhood and served the expedition as a hunter, fisher, and translator. In what is now South Dakota, a Shoshone woman named Sacagawea became part of the expedition.

MINI-BIO

SACAGAWEA: WESTERN AMBASSADOR

Sacagawea (1786?–1812) was a Shoshone born in central Idaho. When she was 12, a band of Hidatsa Indians captured her and took her as a slave. Traded from one village to another, she traveled east until she married a French trader. In 1805, her husband joined the Corps of Discovery led by Lewis and Clark on their journey to the Pacific. Sacagawea and her infant son, Jean Baptiste, joined the expedition. The young woman served as a translator of Indian languages and an ambassador of goodwill. She became key to the expedition's success. When the Corps of Discovery reached Shoshone country, Sacagawea helped them trade for horses. Her presence assured other Shoshones that the expedition came in peace, as no war party ever traveled with a woman and child.

❓ Want to know more? Visit www.factsfornow.scholastic.com and enter the keyword **Idaho**.

Captain Meriwether Lewis and members of his expedition meeting with Shoshones in 1805

Just before entering Idaho, the Corps of Discovery met a traveling band of Shoshones. Sacagawea recognized their leader. It was her own brother, whom she had not seen in five years. Welcoming his long-lost sister, he sold fresh horses to Lewis and Clark and advised them about the best route across the mountains.

The expedition set off on a daunting trek through the Bitterroot Range. One of the men described it in his journal as a "horrible mountainous desert." Game was scarce. At one point, the travelers were so hungry they prepared a meal of dried soup, bear oil, and 20 pounds (9 kilograms) of candles!

At last, on the banks of the Clearwater River, the Corps of Discovery met a group of Nez Perce, who welcomed the half-starved travelers with a feast. In his journal, William Clark wrote, "I find myself very unwell all the evening from eating the fish and roots too freely."

The Corps of Discovery followed the Clearwater to the Snake, and the Snake to the Columbia. In November, the expedition reached the shore of the Pacific, its final destination.

Lewis and Clark returned from their journey with vivid accounts of the country they had seen. They described prairies where huge herds of bison grazed, mountain streams teeming with beavers, and rich fertile land that had never been turned by a farmer's plow. The western territory was a land of immense promise.

IN SEARCH OF THE BEAVER

During the 18th and early 19th centuries, every respectable European gentleman wore a tall felt hat. The felt was

A group of trappers at the start of a beaver hunt

John Jacob Astor

TASTE FOR ADVENTURE

In 1810, Andrew Henry (1775?–1832) and other founders of the Missouri Fur Company built Fort Henry near St. Anthony, Idaho. After a hard winter, they abandoned the fort. Henry returned to the Rockies in 1822, leading a band of William Henry Ashley's trappers. He had several narrow escapes involving grizzly bears and battles with the Blackfoot Indians during his travels in Idaho. In 1824, he left the Rockies to spend the rest of his life mining lead in Missouri.

made from beaver fur. At the same time, beaver capes became fashionable among the wealthy in China. Lewis and Clark's account spurred fur traders to explore Idaho. In 1808, David Thompson of the British North West Company began trapping beaver in the area. The following year, he and two Indian companions built a trading post on Lake Pend Oreille. For the next two years, local Indians brought stacks of glossy beaver pelts to the trading post, called Kullyspell House, and exchanged them for guns, steel knives, iron cooking pots, and rum. Kullyspell House was the first white settlement in present-day Idaho.

Americans were eager to get in on the action. In 1810, the Missouri Fur Company set up a trading post called Fort Henry in today's Fremont County. After a cold, hungry winter and a series of raids by Blackfoot Indians, the traders abandoned the site.

In 1811, John Jacob Astor, a wealthy New York businessman, sent two expeditions to set up a trading post at the mouth of the Columbia River. The first party traveled by sea. The second, led by Wilson Price Hunt, traveled overland. Like Lewis and Clark before them, Hunt and his men ran into difficulties when they entered present-day Idaho. Hunt planned to follow the Snake River to the Columbia and then canoe down the Columbia to the Pacific. But Hunt's party ran into churning rapids on the Snake. One canoe overturned, and a man drowned. As the men struggled on, it became clear that the Snake was too turbulent for canoe travel. Leaving their boats, the men followed the course of the river on foot. One group, led by Donald Mackenzie, left the main party and headed north. Mackenzie reached the Clearwater, built more canoes, and paddled west to the Columbia. His group reached the Pacific a month ahead of Hunt's expedition.

James P. Beckwourth

THE MOUNTAIN MEN

In 1818, Mackenzie returned to Idaho as a trapper with the North West Company. He led a team of Scottish, French Canadian, and Iroquois Indian trappers that came to be called the Snake River Brigade. The brigade set traps in streams and encouraged the local Indians to do the same. Instead of hunting and fishing for food, the Indians spent more and more time trapping beavers and other fur-bearing animals. They were eager to trade for guns and other goods the white men brought.

Competing with the British North West Company (eventually absorbed by the powerful Hudson's Bay Company) was an American enterprise called the Rocky Mountain Fur Company, led by William Henry Ashley. In 1822, Ashley ran a series of newspaper advertisements in eastern cities, seeking men to trap and trade in the

MINI-BIO

COMMANDER NATHANIEL WYETH: THE ICEMAN OF THE MOUNTAINS

As a young man in Massachusetts, Nathaniel Wyeth (1802–1856) ran a business selling blocks of ice. Wyeth was restless, however, and dreamed of heading west. In 1832, he made the first of two trips to the Pacific. He collected hundreds of plant specimens, adding to the scientific knowledge of the plant life of Idaho. In 1834, he founded Fort Hall, which he later sold to the Hudson's Bay Company.

 Want to know more? Visit www.factsfornow .scholastic.com and enter the keyword **Idaho**.

AT THE RENDEZVOUS

The annual rendezvous was the trappers' chance to meet other people and have fun. Men bet on horse races, boxing matches, and card games. They boasted, got into fights, and made up again. The first rendezvous was held in 1825, and the last in 1840. In 1828, it was held at the southern end of Bear Lake. The 1829 and 1832 rendezvous occurred at Pierre's Hole near today's town of Tetonia.

The 1832 rendezvous was in full swing when a band of Blackfoot Indians approached the gathering. The Blackfoot people were enemies of the Nez Perce and other Idaho nations. As they approached, an Indian at the rendezvous shot and killed the Blackfoot chief. The attack sparked a deadly battle that took the lives of at least 10 trappers and their Native friends. No one knows how many Blackfoot people died at the Battle of Pierre's Hole.

Rockies. The notices brought all the men Ashley needed and more. They fanned out across Colorado, Utah, Wyoming, and Idaho to trap beaver, trade with the Indians, and map the new territory.

The trappers lived a quiet existence, working alone or in small, isolated groups. But once a year, they gathered by the hundreds to meet a caravan of supply wagons that rumbled in from St. Louis. The trappers—white, Indian, and black—traded their furs for goods that they would use in the year ahead. This event, called a rendezvous, was not only a time for trade. It was also a chance to feast, play games, and celebrate.

In 1834, by the time a trader named Nathaniel Wyeth arrived at the rendezvous, the mountain men had already bought most of the sup-

Trappers meeting at a rendezvous

plies they needed. Left with wagons full of merchandise, Wyeth set up a trading post at the fork of the Snake and Portneuf rivers north of today's Pocatello. He named the post Fort Hall after one of his fellow traders. The presence of an American fort spurred the British to found a post of their own. Fort Boise in southwestern Idaho was the British answer to Fort Hall.

By 1840, the beaver had disappeared from Idaho's streams, the victims of decades of trapping. The fur trade in Idaho was no longer profitable, and mountain men moved on to other ventures. Yet white people continued flowing into and across the Idaho country.

SPREADING CHRISTIANITY

In 1831, three Nez Perce and a member of the Flathead Nation of Montana made the long journey east to St. Louis to meet with William Clark, who was now the U.S. superintendent of Indian affairs. Using signs, the Indians asked Clark for something. Experts today argue that they probably meant that they wanted to learn how to read and write. But Protestant ministers heard differently—they believed the Indians wanted the Bible to come to them.

The story flew from pulpit to pulpit. Ministers preached sermons about the people of the Northwest who longed to study the word of God. Eager church groups prepared to send **missionaries** to **convert** the Indians to Christianity.

In 1836, Henry and Eliza Spalding set out from St. Louis for Oregon Country. They stopped at a spot on the Clearwater and set up a mission called Lapwai among the Nez Perce people. The Spaldings devoted themselves to converting Nez Perce to Christianity and European American ways. They discouraged hunting and taught the Nez Perce to plant crops. They set up a sawmill for

WORDS TO KNOW

missionaries *people who try to convert others to a religion*

convert *to bring (a person) over from one opinion or belief to another*

CHRISTIAN TEACHER

When Eliza Hart (1807–1851) met Henry Spalding in 1831, she was thrilled to discover that he shared her passion for missionary work. They were married in 1833 and set out for Oregon Country in 1835. With her friend Narcissa Whitman, Eliza became one of the first white women to cross the Rockies into the Northwest. She learned the Nez Perce language and won the Indian women's respect with her gentle, patient ways. For 11 years, she taught at the Lapwai Mission. The Spaldings later settled in Oregon. Eliza became a teacher at Tualatin Academy, which later became Pacific University.

turning logs into lumber, and a gristmill for grinding flour. In 1839, they imported a printing press from Hawai'i, the first in the Northwest. On it they printed portions of the Bible in the Nez Perce language.

Farther up the Clearwater, another missionary couple built a mission at Kamiah. Asa Bowen Smith and his wife, Sarah, lived in the most remote part of Nez Perce country. The Smiths were very interested in the Nez Perce language and culture and made careful notes on everything they observed.

In 1847, an outbreak of measles killed nearly half the population of the Cayuse people around a mission near Walla Walla, Washington. Convinced that the missionaries brought the measles to destroy their people, the Cayuses murdered them. When they heard the news, the Smiths

The arrival of Henry and Eliza Spalding and other members of their party in the Rocky Mountains

A Christian missionary preaching to Native Americans

and the Spaldings abandoned their missions in Idaho. Between 1836 and 1847, they had converted perhaps 20 Indians.

Roman Catholic priests also tried to bring Christianity to the Indians. In the 1840s, Father Pierre-Jean de Smet established a mission among the Coeur d'Alene Indians. In 1850, Father Anthony Ravalli organized a team of Indian laborers and began construction of a mission church overlooking the Coeur d'Alene River. The Cataldo Mission, as the church was named, was completed in 1853.

THE OREGON TRAIL

In 1811, a clerk with Astor's Pacific Fur Company wrote a description of Oregon's Willamette Valley that praised its mild climate and rich soil. Most people made their living

The Cataldo Mission is the oldest building in Idaho. It was built entirely without nails—wooden pegs held its beams together.

FAQ

Q8 WHAT WAS THE OREGON TRAIL?

A8 The Oregon Trail was a 2,000-mile (3,220 km) route from Missouri to Oregon. Between 1840 and 1860, an estimated 500,000 people used it and other trails to go west.

Picture Yourself . . .

Watching Settlers Pass on the Oregon Trail

For months, an endless stream of families, most of them white, has been pouring across your people's ancient hunting grounds. Your parents and adult relatives are shocked by the invasion. Who had ever imagined that so many white people existed! Fortunately, the travelers are not interested in staying in your land. Curious as you are about what's inside their covered wagons, you feel relieved to see them move on.

by farming, and few things were more valuable than rich soil and abundant rain. Lured by the promise of Oregon, thousands of Americans sold their farms and packed up their belongings. They bought teams of oxen and joined a stream of wagon trains heading west. To cross Idaho, they followed the path of the Snake River.

To the people on the Oregon Trail, Idaho was another obstacle. Grass was scarce along the trail, and the oxen grew hungry and thin. Worse still was the thirst. The Snake twisted through a series of high-walled canyons. The parched, weary travelers could see cool water below them, but they could not climb down to reach it.

Fort Hall and Fort Boise were two key way stations along the Oregon Trail in Idaho. There the exhausted travelers stopped for food and rest.

Groups of pioneers traveling on the Oregon Trail

Rider changing horses

They exchanged news with other immigrants and shared their hopes for the future in Oregon.

IDAHO BECOMES AMERICAN

Great Britain and the United States had shared a claim to the Oregon Territory since 1818. As American emigrants poured in, however, the British saw that they were far outnumbered. The fur trade was fading, and the British were losing interest in the Northwest.

In 1846, the United States and Great Britain signed a treaty establishing a clear boundary between U.S. and British territory. Under the treaty, Britain took the land north of the 49th **parallel**, and the United States got the land south of that line. The vast Oregon Territory, including present-day Idaho, was now American.

The trip by oxcart overland from Missouri to Oregon could take as long as six months!

WORD TO KNOW

parallel *a horizontal line on a map or globe; a line of latitude*

A farmer preparing
the soil in north-
ern Idaho for
planting, 1890s

1855

*A group of Mormon
settlers establish
Fort Lemhi on the
Lemhi River*

1860 ▲

*Elias Davidson
Pierce finds gold in
Orofino Creek*

1863

*Idaho becomes a U.S.
territory; U.S. troops
massacre hundreds of
Shoshones at Bear River*

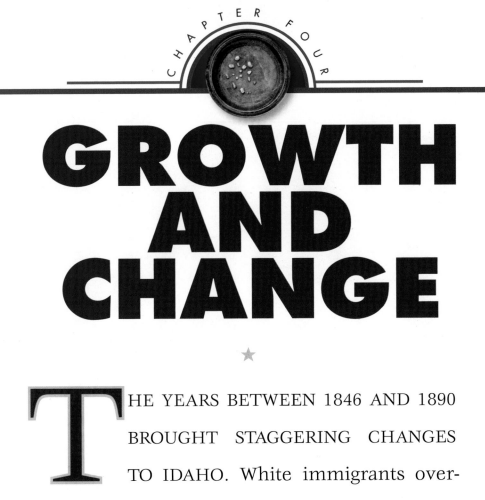

CHAPTER FOUR

GROWTH AND CHANGE

★

THE YEARS BETWEEN 1846 AND 1890 BROUGHT STAGGERING CHANGES TO IDAHO. White immigrants overwhelmed the region's Native people and established settlements across the territory. They planted crops, dug for gold, and changed the landscape forever.

1870

Some 15,000 people live in Idaho Territory

1877

Chief Joseph leads the Oregon band of Nez Perce across Idaho in an effort to escape forced removal to a reservation

◄ **1890**

Idaho becomes the 43rd state

A Mormon family in what is now Idaho, around 1870

THE MORMON SETTLEMENTS

In 1847, a group of Mormons founded a highly successful settlement in Salt Lake City, Utah. New colonies sprang up in many parts of the territory. In 1855, their leader, Brigham Young, sent 27 settlers north into Idaho (which was still part of the Oregon Territory) to convert the Indians and found a settlement. With a herd of cattle and 11 wagons loaded with supplies, Thomas Smith led the settlers to a spot on the Lemhi River, a branch of the Salmon. There they built a **stockade** and dug ditches for **irrigation**. Soon they were busy planting crops and teaching the Indians about Mormonism.

At first, the neighboring Shoshone and Bannock people were friendly, and dozens embraced the new religion. However, trouble flared in the winter of 1858. The Mormons welcomed a visit from a group of Nez Perce,

WORDS TO KNOW

stockade *a fort built with walls of poles driven into the ground*

irrigation *watering land by artificial means to promote plant growth*

enemies of the Shoshone people. The Shoshones felt betrayed. In addition, they were growing concerned that the Mormons planned to start more colonies in their territory. Shoshones attacked the Fort Lemhi settlement, killed two of the settlers, and stole most of their cattle. When word reached Brigham Young, he ordered the surviving settlers back to Utah.

Despite the failure of Fort Lemhi, Mormon settlement continued to spread north into Idaho. In 1860, a group of Mormons led by Thomas Smart established a colony called Franklin at the northern end of the Cache Valley. In the next few years, other settlements sprang up at the southern end of Bear Lake and in the Teton Valley. By 1865, Mormon communities were scattered through much of southern Idaho.

The early Mormon settlers were hardworking farmers. Many came from England and the Scandinavian countries. Some were of African descent. To turn Idaho's sagebrush deserts into cropland, they found ingenious ways to harness the rivers and streams. They built dams to create reservoirs and dug canals to irrigate their fields. Each community centered around a church, and within the first year or two, the families usually built a schoolhouse. Several Mormon towns even had theaters. Farmers with work-calloused hands sat on rough wooden benches to hear the speeches of Shakespeare's Hamlet and Macbeth.

GOLD FEVER

As the Mormon settlers were getting a toehold in Idaho, a very different group of European Americans swarmed into the territory. They had only one purpose in mind: to find gold.

In 1848, a mill foreman named James Marshall saw a sparkle of yellow in a California creek. His discovery

Pan with gold nuggets

Workers at a gold mine at Coeur d'Alene, 1880s

Elias Davidson Pierce

of gold at Sutter's Mill brought a flood of gold seekers to California. In the 1850s, gold fever spread to Oregon. In the summer of 1860, an eager young gold seeker named Elias Davidson Pierce led a band of hopefuls illegally onto Nez Perce land in northern Idaho. In Orofino Creek, a branch of the Clearwater River, they spotted a dreamed-of yellow flash. "Found gold in every place in the stream," Pierce wrote. "I never saw a party of men so much excited. They made the hills and mountains ring with shouts of joy."

Word of the gold strike flew east and west. Within months, gold seekers were tramping up and down northern Idaho. Most traveled by boat up the Columbia, Snake, and Clearwater rivers to the settlement at Lewiston. There they bought pack mules and supplies before they set out to hunt for riches. Gold rush towns sprang up like mushrooms after a rainstorm. By 1862, Idaho had settlements at Pierce City, Orofino, Elk City, Idaho City, Florence, and Warrens (later called Warren).

Among the gold seekers in Oregon Territory were hundreds of men from China. The Chinese had crossed the Pacific to join the California gold rush. Once California's easy gold had been exhausted, they flocked into the Rockies to find fresh diggings. The Chinese were noted for their patience. Often they explored claims that others had abandoned, carefully gathering flecks of gold that the previous miners had overlooked. In 1870, more than a quarter of Idaho's population was Chinese.

Most gold seekers were young men without families. In 1863, Idaho City had a population of 6,267, an estimated 300 of them women. Idaho women opened successful businesses and were respected throughout the territory. Annie Morrow, who lost both feet to frostbite during a winter storm, operated a rooming house in the town of Atlanta. Polly Bemis was a Chinese woman who married an American miner. She ran a boardinghouse in Warrens for many years.

A handful of people struck it rich in Idaho. Jacob Weiser pulled 100 pounds (45 kg) of gold from a creek at Florence in just two days! William Rhodes, who in 1860 became one of the first African Americans to reach

MINI-BIO

POLLY BEMIS: CHINESE PIONEER

Polly Bemis (1853–1933) was born Lalu Nathoy in China. When she was 14, her poverty-stricken parents sold her into slavery. Her master brought her to the United States in the early 1870s to work as a dancer and at a saloon in the mining town of Warrens. By the mid-1880s, Polly bought her freedom and ran a successful boardinghouse. She married Charlie Bemis in 1894, and they moved to a cabin in a remote region of the Salmon River Valley.

? **Want to know more?** Visit www.factsfornow.scholastic.com and enter the keyword **Idaho**.

Between 1861 and 1866, gold seekers are believed to have taken $50 million in gold dust and nuggets from diggings in Idaho.

Q8 WHAT IS THE DIFFERENCE BETWEEN A STATE AND A TERRITORY?

A8 Citizens of a state choose their own governor and state officials. They are eligible to vote in national elections. Senators and representatives from each state vote in Congress. Citizens of a territory cannot vote in national elections and do not have voting representatives in Congress. The federal government appoints the governor of a territory, as well as many territorial officials.

the Clearwater River Basin, left with $80,000. Such tales of overnight wealth lured more gold seekers than ever. Though they collected pocketfuls of gold dust and an occasional nugget, few managed to become rich.

Worth $16 an ounce, gold dust served as currency in the gold rush towns of Idaho. A host of flourishing businesses sopped up the gold that came in from the diggings. Saloon keepers, barbers, tailors, bakers, carpenters, and horse dealers all profited from the hard work of the miners.

BECOMING A TERRITORY

Some of the gold rush towns vanished almost as suddenly as they arose. When the gold ran out, the miners hurried on to new diggings that offered greater promise. Yet Lewiston, Idaho City, and several other communities survived. By 1860, 11,594 residents were scattered over a vast area including today's Washington, Idaho, and western Montana.

In 1859, Oregon joined the Union as a Free State, where slavery was not allowed. The land to the north and east of Oregon formed Washington Territory. From its capital at Olympia, in Washington's northwest corner, the territorial government tried to govern an immense swath of land reaching east to present-day Montana and south to the northern borders of Utah and Nevada. Without railways, telegraphs, or even decent roads, communication with the scattered settlements was almost impossible.

In 1863, Congress carved Idaho from the eastern end of Washington Territory. At first, Lewiston served as the territorial capital. The capital moved south to Boise in 1864. In 1864 and 1868, Congress lopped off territory that became Montana and Wyoming, leaving Idaho with its present boundaries.

Rowdy miners smashing up a saloon

Northern Idaho was a rough-and-tumble area shaped by the lawless spirit of the mining camps. Southern Idaho, in contrast, was a patchwork of Mormon settlements where faith and family were the rule. How did one government manage these two very different Idahos?

In the beginning, the answer seemed to be: not very well. The Idaho Territory was plagued with troubles. Most appointed governors came from the eastern states and did not understand frontier life. Some were corrupt, and some were simply indifferent to the territory's needs. Of the 16 territorial governors appointed between 1863 and 1890, only eight served for a year or more. In the early years, Idaho did not even have an easily enforceable code of criminal laws. **Vigilantes**, bands of citizens who chased down suspects, carried out justice as they saw fit.

Northern Idahoans tended to be rowdy and quarrelsome. The settlers in the south were generally quieter. They were hardworking people who looked to their

WORD TO KNOW

vigilantes *volunteers who decide on their own to stop crime and punish suspected criminals*

U.S. troops pursuing Nez Perce on Dead Mule Trail, 1877

church for guidance. Different as they were, however, the two groups had something in common. Both groups ran into conflict with the Native Americans whose land they had overrun.

FIGHTING FOR THE LAND

Idaho's Indians had endured fur trappers, wagon trains, and hordes of gold seekers. By 1860, the beaver were gone from the streams, horses and cattle had trampled the earth, and gold diggers' spades had pitted the hills. White settlers built permanent houses and fenced in fields to protect their crops. These newcomers planned to stay. By 1870, 15,000 people called Idaho home, including many Chinese immigrants and African Americans.

As game grew scarce, Shoshones in southern Idaho faced starvation. Shoshone bands raided wagon trains, seeking to drive whites away from their territory. In January 1863, U.S. Army colonel Patrick Conner led an attack on a Shoshone encampment on the Bear River.

Badly outnumbered, the Shoshones suffered a decisive defeat. Hundreds of men, women, and children were slaughtered. The Bear River Massacre, as it is known today, was the worst Indian massacre in U.S. history.

The massacre broke the spirit of the Shoshone people, who lost most of their land through treaties with the U.S. government. Shoshones, Bannocks, and Northern Paiutes were forced onto the Fort Hall Indian Reservation. There was little game, and Indians had to depend on the government for food and clothing.

In 1855, Idaho's Nez Perce people signed a treaty creating a large reservation in the Clearwater Valley. After Elias Pierce found gold on Nez Perce land, however, the reservation was whittled down from 11,000 to 1,000 square miles (28,500 to 2,600 sq km).

The western band of Nez Perce, who lived in the Wallowa Mountains of Oregon, had not signed any treaties. In 1877, the U.S. Army ordered the Oregon Nez Perce to leave their homeland and move to the reservation in Idaho. Their leader, known by whites as Chief Joseph, led his people on a heroic and daring escape. For more than three months, the army pursued Chief Joseph and his people across Idaho and into Montana. They were finally surrounded within 40 miles (64 km) of the Canadian border. As he surrendered, Chief Joseph gave a moving speech. "It is cold and we have no blankets," he said simply. "The little children are freezing to death. . . . My heart is sick and sad. From where the sun now stands I will fight no more forever."

GROWING TOWARD STATEHOOD

In the 1880s, railroads finally reached the territory, winding through the mountains to bring mail, supplies, and more settlers. Railroads made the mining of silver, lead, and other

SHERIFF BY A HAIR

In the 1870 election for sheriff of Boise, Lute Lindsey claimed he had defeated William Bryon by one vote. But Bryon discovered that election officials had refused to count the votes of three African Americans. After the three men swore on a Bible they voted for Bryon, the judge declared Bryon the new sheriff by two votes.

Chief Joseph

Idaho: From Territory to Statehood

(1863–1890)

This map shows the original Idaho Territory and the area (in yellow) that became the state of Idaho in 1890.

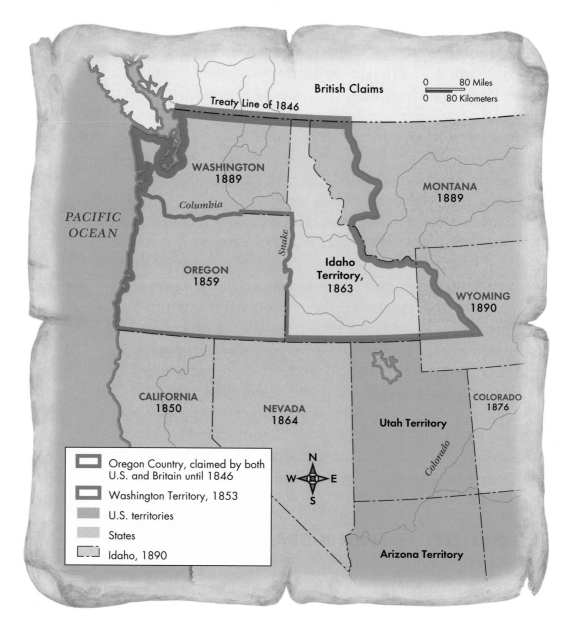

minerals more profitable. The railroads brought miners and equipment, and carried valuable ore to market. Sheep also became profitable, and young Basque men came to Idaho to work as shepherds. The mountains resembled their homeland in the Pyrenees Mountains between Spain and France.

Northern Idahoans tended to be suspicious of southern Idaho's Mormons. They argued that Mormons voted as a block, taking their orders from church leaders in Utah. Much anti-Mormon feeling focused on the Mormon practice of some men taking more than one wife at the same time, a practice called plural marriage.

In 1884, a new law required Mormons to sign the Idaho Test Oath in order to vote in any territorial election. The oath stated that the signer did not practice plural marriage or support it. Since few Mormons were willing to sign the oath, they could not be represented in the territorial legislature.

In the spring of 1890, a group of delegates from Idaho's non-Mormon communities gathered in Boise to draw up a state constitution. The document set up the rules for state government and upheld the Idaho Test Oath Act. The U.S. Congress reviewed the proposed constitution in June. Mormons supported the Democratic Party, whereas most non-Mormons were Republican. Eager to bring another Republican state into the Union, Republicans in Congress hastily approved the Idaho Constitution, and Idaho became a state on July 3.

The largest population of people of Basque descent in the United States is in and around Boise.

READ ABOUT

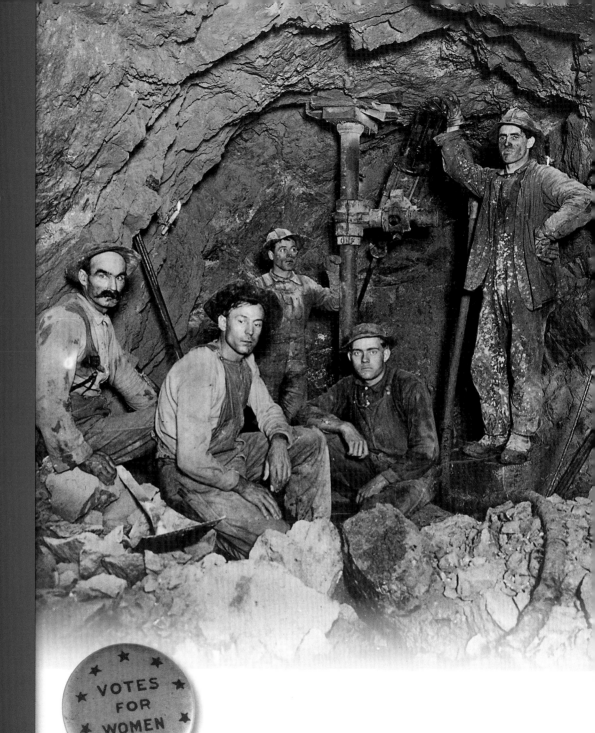

Workers in a lead
mine in the Coeur
d'Alene region,
early 1900s

VOTES FOR WOMEN

1896 ▲

*Women in Idaho
win the right to vote*

1899

*Governor Frank
Steunenberg calls in
troops to end violent
protests at mines*

1910

*The "Big Burn"
destroys 3 million
acres (1.2 million ha)
of forest in northern
Idaho*

MORE MODERN TIMES

CHAPTER FIVE

MORE MODERN TIMES

★

POWERFUL GROUPS IN DISTANT CITIES CONTROLLED THE WAGES AND WORKING CONDITIONS OF IDAHO MINERS. Businessmen such as Cyrus McCormick and John D. Rockefeller Jr. made millions by investing in Idaho mines. But miners in the Coeur d'Alene Mountains earned as little as $3.50 for a 10-hour day. With few safety measures in place, miners were often injured or killed on the job.

1942–1945

Japanese Americans are held prisoner at Minidoka detention camp

1976

The Teton Dam collapses

2013 ▲

Wildfires rage in southern and southwestern Idaho

U.S. troops camping at a mine in Wallace during the conflicts of 1892

WORDS TO KNOW

martial law *law carried out by military forces*

suffrage *the right to vote*

philanthropist *a person who helps others by giving time and money to causes and charities*

THE RICHES OF THE EARTH

When silver prices tumbled in 1892, mine owners slashed wages still further. Outraged workers marched into the town of Gem and dynamited a silver mill. Idaho's governor declared **martial law**. Idaho National Guardsmen and federal troops marched into Gem and arrested hundreds of protesting miners. Many were jailed for up to two years. But they came home as heroes to their families and fellow miners.

During the 1890s, most Idaho mine workers banded together to demand better wages and safer working conditions. But the owners of the Bunker Hill and Sullivan Mine prevented their workers from joining the union, called the Western Federation of Miners (WFM). On April 29,

1899, frustrated miners marched on the mine and blew up some of its equipment. Governor Frank Steunenberg called in the military once more. Hundreds of miners were arrested, and the strength of the WFM in the state was broken.

By 1905, Steunenberg had left politics. One December night, a bomb exploded and killed him. The police believed that Steunenberg had been murdered in revenge for his actions against the WFM. They arrested a miner named Albert Horsley, who confessed. He claimed he'd had the help of three union leaders from Colorado. The nation's top civil liberties lawyer Clarence Darrow defended the union leaders at their trial. He raised such serious questions about Horsley's truthfulness, and his being coached and pressured by the police and prosecution, that the union leaders were set free. Horsley was convicted and spent the rest of his life in prison.

WINNING THE VOTE

In 1890, the Mormon Church ended its support of plural marriage. Three years later, the Idaho State Legislature removed its restrictions against Mormon voters.

Women, too, fought for the right to vote in Idaho elections. Traveling by riverboat, stagecoach, and horseback, Abigail Scott Duniway gave several speeches on suffrage in Idaho between 1876 and 1895. In 1896, Idaho became

MINI-BIO

MAY ARKWRIGHT HUTTON: FROM RAGS TO RICHES

In the 1880s, May Arkwright Hutton (1860–1915) moved to the Idaho Panhandle to work as a cook in the mining camps. She and her husband scraped together enough savings to buy a share in the Hercules Mine. In 1901, miners discovered a valuable vein of silver and lead. Suddenly, the Huttons were rich. They moved to Spokane, Washington, in 1906, and May became a leader in the struggle for woman suffrage. She never forgot her humble beginnings and died a beloved philanthropist.

? **Want to know more?** Visit www.factsfornow.scholastic.com and enter the keyword **Idaho**.

FAQ

Q8 WHAT WERE THE FIRST FOUR U.S. STATES TO GIVE WOMEN THE RIGHT TO VOTE?

A8 Wyoming, Colorado, Utah, and Idaho were the first U.S. states to allow women to vote.

MINI-BIO

ABIGAIL SCOTT DUNIWAY: FIGHTER FOR WOMEN'S RIGHTS

As a young teacher on the Oregon frontier, Abigail Scott Duniway (1834–1915) was outraged that women earned far less than men for the same work. She believed that in order to receive equal treatment, women needed the right to vote. She spoke for woman suffrage throughout the Northwest and spent much of her time trying to secure the vote for women in Idaho. After Idaho women succeeded in 1896, Duniway worked in Oregon for woman suffrage. In 1912, she became the first woman to register to vote in that state.

? Want to know more? Visit www.factsfornow.scholastic.com and enter the keyword **Idaho**.

WORD TO KNOW

magnate *a person with money and power, especially someone in industry*

the fourth state to give women the right to vote.

THE WEALTH OF THE FORESTS

In 1900, a lumber **magnate** named Frederick Weyerhaeuser bought vast tracts of Idaho's pine forest. Axes rang out in the once quiet woods, and mighty, centuries-old trees groaned and crashed to the ground. Other companies rushed to get in on the profits. The loggers moved on to fresh forests, leaving a wreckage of stumps in their wake.

The summer of 1910 was one of the driest on record. Forest underbrush withered, died, and turned into tinder. Lightning strikes set brush fires all across northern Idaho. By early August, hundreds of small fires merged into a sweeping storm of smoke and flames. The "Big Burn," as it is called today, destroyed 3 million acres (1.2 million ha) of Idaho forests. Eighty-five people, many of them firefighters, were killed before late-summer rainstorms put out the flames.

As the years passed, some Idaho timber companies began to see the need for long-term planning. Instead of cutting down entire forests, they selected some trees to harvest and left the others standing. They also planted new trees in areas that had been logged. Such efforts kept the forests healthy and ensured a timber supply for generations to come.

Lumber loaded along rails in an Idaho forest, 1890s

MINI-BIO

EDWARD PULASKI: HERO OF THE BIG BURN

When the Big Burn broke out in 1910, U.S. Forest Service ranger Edward Pulaski (1868–1931) was in charge of a firefighting crew near the town of Wallace. His crew was powerless against the fire, and their lives were in grave danger. Pulaski led his men into an abandoned mine shaft. He stood at the entrance, beating away the flames as the fire roared past. Thirty-eight of his 43 men survived the ordeal. He also invented the Pulaski, a tool that has an axe blade on one side and a hoe on the other. Firefighters use it to chop away trees and underbrush and to dig trenches to stop oncoming flames.

? Want to know more? Visit www.factsfornow.scholastic.com and enter the keyword **Idaho**.

Like Idaho's miners, loggers in the Gem State struggled for better wages and working conditions. In 1914, Idaho's governor, Moses Alexander, signed laws that gave loggers higher wages and eight-hour workdays.

WATERING THE LAND

When pioneers crossed Idaho on the Oregon Trail, no one could have imagined the deserts rippling with wheat and alfalfa. But with irrigation, Mormon farmers turned the desert into rich farmland. In the early 20th century, a series of gigantic dams on the Snake and Boise rivers created reservoirs and channeled water to some of the

In 1925, the town of American Falls was moved to a new location to make room for the American Falls Dam. When the dam was finished, the old town was flooded. When water in the reservoir is low, you can see some buildings of the old town.

WORD TO KNOW

foreclosure *a legal process for taking back property when the payment for it is overdue*

state's thirstiest areas. Irrigation created millions of acres of fertile farmland and grazing land for herds of cattle and sheep. Farmers grew wheat, corn, and alfalfa. Beans, onions, sugar beets, and potatoes became highly profitable crops.

HARD TIMES

During World War I (1914–1918), Idaho farms benefited from the demand for wheat, potatoes, and other food to feed factory workers and troops. In the early 1920s, however, prices for farm produce collapsed. Potatoes, which sold for $1.51 a bushel in 1919, brought only 30 cents a bushel in 1922. As a series of droughts added to their troubles, the farmers struggled to keep going.

In the 1930s, the nation sank into its worst economic depression. Banks failed, factories closed, and millions of people lost their jobs. Idaho farmers were hard-hit as prices tumbled lower than ever. Thousands of farmers could not meet payments on loans, and lost their land and homes through **foreclosure**.

President Franklin D. Roosevelt tried to help Americans secure jobs and avoid starvation through a series of programs called the New Deal. The Civilian Conservation Corps (CCC) gave jobs to young men. About 20,000 men worked on CCC projects in Idaho. They cleared trails and set up campgrounds in state and national parks. They built bridges, fences, and roads. Men and women hired by the Works Progress Administration (WPA) and other New Deal programs built schools, fairgrounds, airports, and sewer systems.

For Idahoans, one of the most exciting New Deal programs was the Rural Electrification Administration (REA). Work crews strung wire to pocket-sized towns and isolated farmhouses throughout the state. For

Members of the Civilian Conservation Corps work on a truck trail in Selway National Forest, 1930s

the first time, lights flicked on at the touch of a switch, music and news poured from radios, and rural Idahoans drew closer to the world outside.

During the Depression years, thousands of people left Idaho to search for work in other states. However, many people moved into the Gem State from Oklahoma and Kansas, where times were even harder. Some young men who came to Idaho with the CCC decided to make the Gem State their permanent home. As one former CCC worker explained, "I was infected by a contagious bug called Idaho mountain fever and it was just too pleasant to leave."

MINI-BIO

VERNON BAKER: IDAHO WAR HERO

During World War II, Vernon Baker (1919–2010) led an attack against German forces barricaded in an Italian castle. His action was worthy of a Congressional Medal of Honor, the highest award a veteran can receive. But Baker was black, and Congress was reluctant to grant the award to African Americans. It took Congress until 1997 to give Lieutenant Baker his due. The medal's citation said, "Lt. Baker's fighting spirit and daring leadership were an inspiration to his men and exemplify the highest traditions of the armed forces."

? **Want to know more?** Visit www.factsfornow .scholastic.com and enter the keyword **Idaho**.

When World War II broke out, Idaho potatoes and other vegetables helped feed the U.S. Army. Every year during the war, Idaho's J. R. Simplot Company alone shipped 33 million pounds (15 million kg) of potatoes to the troops.

THE SHADOW OF WAR

On December 7, 1941, Japanese planes destroyed the U.S. naval fleet at Pearl Harbor in Hawai'i in a surprise attack. The United States declared war on Japan and also on its allies, Germany and Italy. The war created markets for Idaho's many farm products and minerals. Mines operated around the clock, producing lead, zinc, tungsten, and other minerals needed to make weapons and other military equipment. U.S. Air Force training fields opened at Boise, Gowen Field, and Mountain Home. Lake Pend Oreille became the site of the Farragut Naval Training Base, the nation's second-largest naval training station.

From the start of the war, some people spread fears that Japanese Americans might be spies sending secret information to Japan. In February 1942, President Roosevelt ordered that all Japanese Americans be removed from the West Coast and southern Arizona, and held at detention centers. One of these centers, Minidoka, was located near Hunt, Idaho. The first of some 10,000 men, women, and children arrived at Minidoka in August. They were held at this camp against their will and without charges or trials. None had committed any crimes, and they all were loyal Americans.

Most of Idaho's young men were fighting overseas, and farmers faced a severe labor shortage. In 1942, Japanese American workers were recruited from Minidoka. Idaho

Japanese American farmworkers in the fields of a Farm Security Administration camp in Twin Falls County, 1942

farmers had already depended for decades on Mexican migrant labor, and in 1942, the U.S. and Mexican governments agreed on a formal program for Mexican laborers, called *braceros*, to work on American farms. From 1942 to 1946, more than 15,000 braceros worked Idaho fields. Without Mexican and Japanese American labor, large swaths of Idaho crop fields would have been wasted.

In 1945, the United States dropped the world's first atomic bombs on the Japanese cities of Hiroshima and Nagasaki. The bombings ended the war with Japan, and the prisoners at Minidoka went home.

WORD TO KNOW

geologists *scientists who study the history of Earth*

FROM FIELDWORK TO THE BENCH

The son of Mexican migrant farmworkers, Sergio A. Gutierrez dropped out of high school to go to work and help his family. In his 20s, he moved to Idaho and finished high school through a program at Boise State University. He went on to earn a law degree. In 2002, Gutierrez was elected to the Idaho Court of Appeals, becoming the first Latino to hold such a high position in the state judicial system.

POSTWAR CHANGES

A growing market and improved farming methods brought boom times to Idaho's farmers in the 1950s. **Geologists** found that Idaho had rich deposits of phosphate, a mineral used in chemical fertilizers. With the combination of fertilizers and irrigation, Idaho fields yielded bumper crops. Idaho came to lead the nation in potato production. Farmers needed labor to fuel this boom, so the bracero program continued—along with some white farmers' racist attitudes toward their Mexican workers.

Mexicans' wages were much lower than wages paid to white workers. Latinos also struggled with poor schools and limited access to health care. When the bracero program ended in the 1960s, U.S. secretary of labor Lee G. Williams called it "legalized slavery."

On September 20, 1974, the Kutenai Indians made headlines by declaring war against the United States. In the 1930s, the federal government had taken their ancestral land from them, and they lived in dire poverty near Bonners Ferry. After years of pleading for help, chairwoman Amy Trice declared war as a means of making the public aware of her people's plight. The Kutenai set up a tollbooth on the state highway, and teens collected 10-cent tolls for the Kutenai cause. "The boys did some drumming and singing," Trice said later. "Word got out we were on the war path . . . they thought we were getting ready to attack!" After two weeks, the Bureau of Indian Affairs met with the Kutenai and set aside 12.5 acres (5 ha) for the tribe.

Meanwhile, Idaho farmers continued to depend on cheap Mexican labor, and the 1980s and 1990s saw a huge influx of Latino immigrants. The state's Latino population grew from about 36,560 in 1980 to more than 100,000 in 2006. In 2003, Latinos and Native Americans

A teenager working in a sugar beet field in southwest Idaho

in Idaho joined forces to form the Tribal Latino Caucus. Recognizing that they faced many common problems, the groups began working together to gain political power in the state.

The town of Sugar City was flooded after the Teton Dam burst in 1976.

Q8 HAS THERE EVER BEEN A SERIOUS NUCLEAR ACCIDENT AT THE INL?

A8 On January 3, 1961, an experimental reactor called SL-1 exploded, killing three workers at the site. The deaths in the SL-1 explosion are the only known fatalities from a nuclear accident in the United States.

ENVIRONMENTAL RESPONSIBILITIES

When the United States used atomic bombs on Japan in World War II, it launched the world into an era of frightening new weapons. Many people, however, hoped that atomic, or nuclear, power could be harnessed for peaceful purposes as well. In 1949, the U.S. government opened what is now known as the Idaho National Laboratory (INL) on a large tract of desert between Idaho Falls and Arco. Scientists at the INL work to develop nuclear energy to produce electricity and fuel submarines.

Though mining, farming, and logging brought jobs and profits to Idaho, these industries took a heavy toll on the state's environment. In the 1960s and 1970s, environmentalists called for the cleanup of polluted rivers and preservation of wilderness areas.

When plans were launched for a new dam on the Teton River, many environmentalists worried that it would destroy the river's wildlife. Completed in the fall of 1975, the Teton Dam was intended to provide flood control and irrigation, and to generate electric power. On the morning of June

5, 1976, inspectors noticed water gushing through a hole on one side of the dam. Then, with a mighty roar, the entire dam collapsed into the river. Eighty billion gallons (300 billion liters) of water burst from the reservoir and raged down the Upper Snake River Valley. The rampaging water destroyed hundreds of homes in Rexburg, Sugar City, Idaho City, and other towns in its path. The flood took 11 lives and caused more than $500 million in property damage.

Environmental issues played a key role in the 1970 race for governor. Cecil D. Andrus was elected on a promise to fight molybdenum mining in the White Cloud Mountains. Environmentalists rejoiced in 1980 when 2.3 million acres (931,000 ha) of land were set aside as the River of No Return Wilderness Area.

Idaho's forests and wilderness areas became the subject of national news headlines in 2013 when dozens of wildfires burned throughout the southern and southwestern parts of the state. In August alone, more than 250,000 acres (101,000 ha) burned, forcing thousands of residents to evacuate and endangering local wildlife. Hundreds of homes were destroyed. A lightning strike at Beaver Creek started a fire that burned for three weeks before firefighters could contain it. The cost of fighting the Beaver Creek fire was more than $24 million.

MINI-BIO

BARBARA MORGAN: TEACHER IN SPACE

On August 8, 2007, Barbara Morgan (1951–), a second- and third-grade teacher from McCall-Donnelly Elementary School, lifted into space aboard the space shuttle Endeavour. She was the first teacher to complete a successful mission as part of NASA's Teacher in Space program. From the International Space Station, Morgan spoke by radio with schoolchildren at the Discovery Center of Idaho in Boise. Her adventure in space inspired young people throughout the United States, especially children in her native state of Idaho.

? **Want to know more?** Visit www.factsfornow .scholastic.com and enter the keyword **Idaho**.

Firefighters battle flames near Bliss in July 2013.

72

READ ABOUT

Fans cheer for the
Boise State University
football team during
a 2013 game.

CHAPTER SIX

PEOPLE

★

"THE PEOPLE OF IDAHO LIKE SMALL TOWNS, AND THEY LIKE FREE SPACE," WRITER A. B. GUTHRIE SAID. "They fill their eyes with grandeur and their ears with the great silence of the mountains." Idaho is a state with much to offer, and its people still cherish the outdoors and feel deep ties to their history.

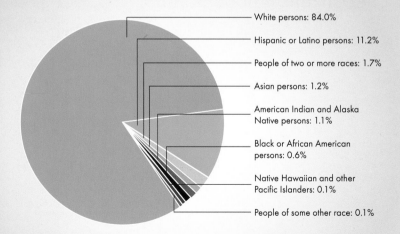

People QuickFacts

White persons: 84.0%

Hispanic or Latino persons: 11.2%

People of two or more races: 1.7%

Asian persons: 1.2%

American Indian and Alaska Native persons: 1.1%

Black or African American persons: 0.6%

Native Hawaiian and other Pacific Islanders: 0.1%

People of some other race: 0.1%

Source: U.S. Census Bureau, 2010 census

Idahoans at a barbecue picnic at Sandy Point near Boise

CITY LIFE AND COUNTRY LIFE

Idaho's biggest city is Boise, but other cities such as Nampa and Pocatello have experienced recent growth. More and more people move to Idaho each day, making it one of the fastest-growing states in the country.

Where Idahoans Live

The colors on this map indicate population density throughout the state.
The darker the color, the more people live there.

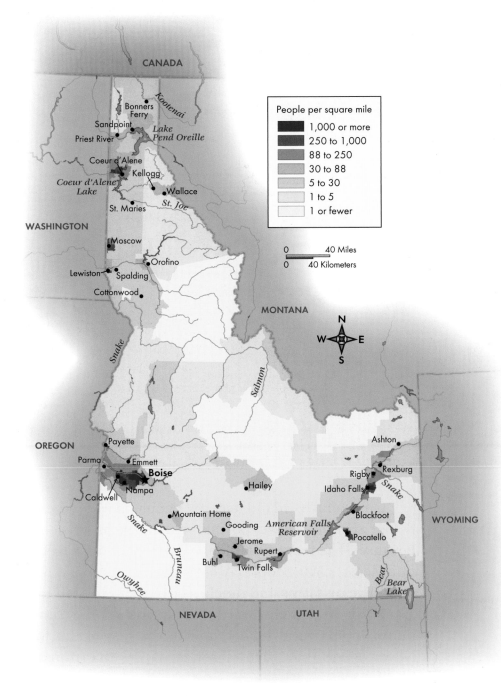

People per square mile

■	1,000 or more
■	250 to 1,000
■	88 to 250
■	30 to 88
■	5 to 30
■	1 to 5
☐	1 or fewer

0   40 Miles
0   40 Kilometers

Horseback riding in one of Idaho's many natural areas

Idaho has a smaller population than the city of Houston, Texas!

On average, Idaho has 19 people per square mile (7 per sq km). However, this figure can be misleading, because 71 percent of all Idahoans live in cities or towns of at least 2,500 people. A very sizable number (29 percent) live on farms and ranches or in tiny, isolated towns.

Roads and highways, telephones, and the Internet help connect rural Idahoans with the rest of the world. Nevertheless, they live closer to nature than most city

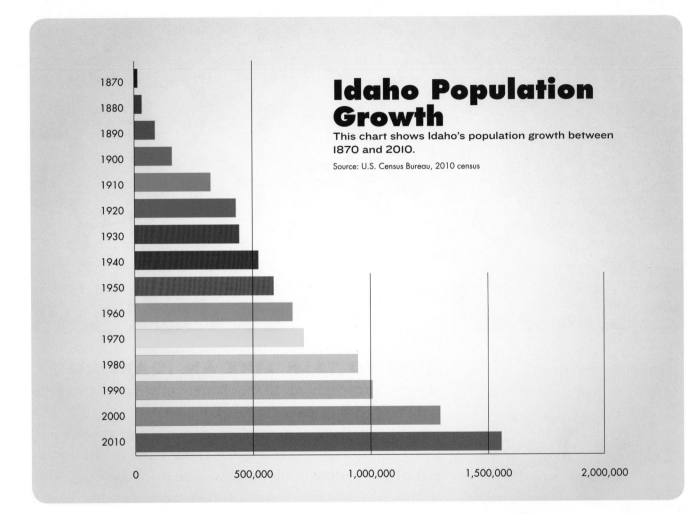

Idaho Population Growth

This chart shows Idaho's population growth between 1870 and 2010.

Source: U.S. Census Bureau, 2010 census

dwellers can imagine. Their lives often revolve around planting and harvesting crops or caring for sheep, cattle, and horses.

Whether they live in a Boise condo or a farmhouse in the Snake River Valley, most Idahoans love the outdoors. Ski slopes and trout streams are within an hour's drive of Boise and Pocatello. On the weekends, many Idahoans like to pack up their camping gear and head into the mountains. They enjoy biking, boating, horseback riding, and hiking. Outdoor Idaho is everyone's backyard.

Big City Life

This list shows the population of Idaho's biggest cities.

Boise. 205,671
Nampa. 81,557
Meridian 75,092
Idaho Falls. 56,813
Pocatello 54,255

Source: U.S. Census Bureau, 2010 census

Gourds and fresh produce for sale at a farmers' market in Fruitland

IDAHO POTATOES

The "Idaho potato" is the russet Burbank. It is large and white, and has a slightly rough skin. The botanist Luther Burbank developed it in 1914.

HOW TO TALK LIKE AN IDAHOAN

Sonja Launspach of Idaho State University directs a long-term study called the Idaho Dialect Project. The project reveals that a number of words and speech patterns are unique to parts of the Gem State. In southeastern Idaho, people tend to pronounce an "a" before verbs: "I was a-waiting for you" or "We were a-sitting here." "Way up down" means "very far down." Other unique Idaho words include "sluffing" (skipping school), "jockey box" (glove compartment), and "borrow pit" (dip alongside a road).

HOW TO EAT LIKE AN IDAHOAN

Idaho farms, ranches, and orchards produce a wealth of great things to eat. Generations of Idaho cooks have developed recipes using wheat, barley, berries, asparagus, lamb, apples, and, of course, that all-time Idaho favorite, the potato!

★ MENU ★

WHAT'S ON THE MENU IN IDAHO?

★ ★ ★

Lamb barley soup

Lamb Barley Soup

A soup using a beef broth with lamb chunks, vegetables, and barley. It can easily be a meal in itself!

Pickled Asparagus

Asparagus pickled with vinegar, salt, onion, and spices. It makes a delicious appetizer.

Deer Chop Hurry

Thinly sliced venison chops browned in a skillet and then slow-cooked with onions and brown sugar.

Asparagus

Apple Crunch Pie

A traditional apple pie with a yummy topping made from oatmeal and pecans.

The Not-So-Lowly Potato

Idaho potatoes are not only delicious, they're also good for you! According to the Idaho Potato Commission, one potato gives you 18 percent of the potassium and 45 percent of the vitamin C you need daily.

TRY THIS RECIPE
Basic Twice-Baked Idaho Potatoes

Here's a delicious way to enjoy Idaho potatoes. Have an adult nearby in case you need help.

Ingredients:
4 large Idaho potatoes (8 to 10 ounces each)
½ cup light sour cream or yogurt
1 pinch nutmeg
Salt and freshly ground pepper to taste
Milk (as desired)
½ cup grated Parmesan cheese

Instructions:
1. Wash the potatoes and pierce them with a fork.
2. Bake the potatoes in a microwave on "potato" setting, or in a conventional oven at 425°F for 1 hour.
3. Hold the hot potatoes with an oven mitt and cut them lengthwise. Carefully scoop out the inside into a medium-sized bowl, leaving the shell about ¼-inch thick.
4. Mash the potato flesh in the bowl with a potato masher.
5. Add sour cream or yogurt, nutmeg, and salt and pepper. Mash until smooth, adding a little milk if necessary to make a smooth consistency. Stir in the cheese.
6. Using a spoon, gently fill the potato shells with the potato mixture, mounding it up high.
7. Place the filled potatoes on a baking sheet and bake at 400°F for 18 to 20 minutes.
8. Dig in!

Kindergarten students learn to write in Chinese at a school in Meridian.

GOING TO SCHOOL

A group of Nez Perce children were the first pupils to attend school in Idaho. They were enrolled at the Lapwai Mission School founded by Henry and Eliza Spalding in 1836. Mormon settlers in southern Idaho set up schools for their children, and education has been an important part of Idaho life ever since. In 2012, 251,712 students were enrolled in 703 public schools from kindergarten through 12th grade. About 18,000 children were enrolled in charter schools.

Today, some 12,500 students pursue undergraduate and graduate degrees at the University of Idaho. The university is noted for programs in animal science, forestry, law, theater arts, and wildlife resources. Other major universities in the state include Idaho State University at Pocatello and Boise State University at Boise.

TELLING THE STORY

Mourning Dove, a Salish Indian, was one of the first novelists born in Idaho. She was born near Bonner's Ferry in the 1880s. When she was a child, her family left Idaho, and she grew up in Washington. Her book *Cogewea, the Half-Blood* appeared in 1927 and is regarded as the first novel ever written by a Native American woman.

Wallace Thurman grew up in Boise before he moved to New York City to become part of the Harlem Renaissance. In his novel *The Blacker the Berry*, he recalled his easy, friendly social life as an African American in Idaho. "White and black women talked over the back fences and lent one another needed household commodities."

Many of the novels of Vardis Fisher, born in Annis, reflect his lonely, troubled childhood on an isolated farm. *Children of God* (1939) is the story of a Mormon community on the Idaho frontier.

Lured by mountains and big rivers, Glenn Balch moved from Texas to Idaho after he graduated from college. His experiences in the Sawtooth and Owyhee mountains inspired many of his books for young readers. *Tiger Roan* (1938) is told from the point of view of a wild horse that is captured and trained for the rodeo.

Ernest Hemingway's career as a writer was well established when he moved to Ketchum in the 1930s. He loved hunting, canoeing, and rafting, and Idaho provided him with all of these and other outdoor

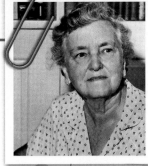

MINI-BIO

CAROL RYRIE BRINK: STORYTELLER

Orphaned as a child, Carol Ryrie Brink (1895–1981) grew up with her grandmother in Moscow, Idaho. Her grandmother's stories of frontier life in Wisconsin are the background for Brink's novel for children, *Caddie Woodlawn*, which won the Newbery Medal in 1936. Some of her other books include *The Highly Trained Dogs of Professor Petit* (1953) and *Winter Cottage* (1968).

❓ Want to know more? Visit www.factsfornow.scholastic.com and enter the keyword **Idaho**.

Pulitzer Prize–winning writer Marilynne Robinson was born and raised in Sandpoint.

REMEMBERING HER HERITAGE

The daughter of a Coeur d'Alene father and a Kutenai-Irish mother, Janet Campbell Hale (1947–) lived for a time on the Coeur d'Alene reservation in Idaho while she was growing up. As a teenager, she began to write poems and stories as an escape from poverty and family strife. *The Owl's Song* (1974) examines many forms of racial prejudice. Her autobiography, *Bloodlines: Odyssey of a Native Daughter*, was published in 1993.

adventures. Hemingway, who received the Nobel Prize in Literature, wrote his great novel of the Spanish civil war, *For Whom the Bell Tolls* (1939), at the Sun Valley Lodge.

Another award-winning writer is Marilynne Robinson of Sandpoint, who won the Pulitzer Prize in 2005 for her novel *Gilead*. The Gem State is the setting of her first novel, *Housekeeping* (1981). The book takes place in a fictional town called Fingerbone on the shores of a lake not unlike Lake Pend Oreille.

THINGS OF BEAUTY

Life on the Idaho frontier left little time for painting and sculpture. However, a handful of women and men managed to pursue their passion for art. Margaretta Favorite Brown painted portraits of Idaho settlers and scenes of life in the mining camps. Like Brown, Charles Ostner arrived in Idaho in 1862. He set up a ferry service on the Payette River. When business slowed during the winter, he carved statues from wood. His life-sized statue of George Washington on horseback stands in the Idaho state capitol today. For his model, Ostner used the portrait of Washington on a postage stamp!

The forests and mountains of the Gem State are an inspiration to many Idaho artists. James Palmersheim of Moscow creates detailed landscapes in pastels. Romey Stuckart, who moved to Hope in 1980, paints large canvases of forest scenes. In 1992, Stuckart's work brought her a Guggenheim Fellowship, one of the highest awards given to artists in the United States.

Many Idaho artists use local materials. Dennis Sullivan carves statues from the wood of ponderosa pines that grow on his land near Cottonwood. Sullivan specializes in "finding the dog beneath the bark," carving canines of all shapes and sizes. His wife, Frances Conklin, paints each new dog as it is finished.

Born to Danish immigrant parents in a cabin near Bear Lake, John Gutzon de la Mothe Borglum (also known as Gutzon Borglum) studied sculpture in San Francisco and New York, and later in Europe. In 1927, he began his life's greatest work, a colossal sculpture at Mount Rushmore in South Dakota depicting the faces of

REINVENTING THE BOOK

Throughout his life, James Castle (1899–1977) made books by stitching together sheets of scrap paper. He covered the pages with drawings in ink that he made from soot and ground-up bits of colored paper. On some pages, he made lines of symbols, which were apparently his own invented writing system. Castle had never learned to read. He was deaf from birth, and teachers believed he could not be taught. He lived his entire life in rural Idaho, but today his work is celebrated in galleries across the nation.

Painted gourds
for sale in Boise

U.S. presidents George Washington, Thomas Jefferson, Abraham Lincoln, and Theodore Roosevelt. Borglum died before the work was complete, and the finishing touches were added by his son Lincoln Borglum.

MAKING MUSIC

Ever since the 1910s, the Idaho town of Weiser has held contests for the state's best fiddlers. The competitions gave rise to the National Oldtime Fiddlers' Contest in the 1950s. The contest is held in June and brings more than 20,000 people to the town.

The Idaho State Civic Symphony gave its first peformances at the start of the 20th century. The Coeur d'Alene Symphony, the Meridian Symphony, and the Idaho Choral Symphony Orchestra (based in Boise) are other leading orchestras in the state.

Artist Gutzon Borglum working on a clay model of Mount Rushmore

Musicians Joe Lovano (right) and Christian McBride at the 2001 Lionel Hampton International Jazz Festival

The University of Idaho in Moscow plays host to the Lionel Hampton International Jazz Festival each February. Jazz great Lionel Hampton began playing at the festival in 1984 and it was later named for him. Over the years, musicians such as Ella Fitzgerald, Dizzy Gillespie, Diana Krall, and Wynton Marsalis have performed there.

MINI-BIO

MARK LINDSAY: ROCK AND ROLL STAR

Mark Lindsay (1942–) grew up in Wilder and began performing with local bands in high school. He was the lead singer and saxophone player in a group called the Downbeats, which also included his friend Paul Revere and others. As a gimmick, Lindsay and Revere decided to change their band's name to Paul Revere and the Raiders. Success came quickly, with hit records such as "Kicks" and "Hungry" and countless TV appearances. Lindsay went on to a thriving solo career, making records and performing in concert.

? **Want to know more?** Visit www.factsfornow .scholastic.com and enter the keyword **Idaho.**

A snowboarder in Sun Valley

SEE IT HERE!

SUN VALLEY

In 1936, W. Averell Harriman, chief executive of the Union Pacific Railroad, was looking for a way to encourage tourism in the western states. He hit on a plan to develop a ski resort in the mountains near Ketchum, Idaho. Sun Valley pioneered the use of the chairlift for carrying skiers up the mountains, and it opened the world's first child-sized cross-country tracks. Today, the old Union Pacific Railroad tracks have been turned into a 30-mile (48 km) Wood River Trail system, which ends in Sun Valley.

SPORTS

The natural beauty of Idaho encourages outdoor sports of all kinds. Skiing, biking, and hiking are popular pastimes for Idahoans.

Early in the 20th century, the track and basketball teams of the University of Idaho soared to national fame. Coaching the teams was Olympic track-and-field star Clarence "Hec" Edmundson. His legacy of excellence continues at the University of Idaho.

Today, the University of Idaho, Idaho State, and Boise State have powerhouse basketball and football teams. And the rivalries among teams are strong.

PICABO STREET: FROM TRIUMPH TO TRIUMPH

Growing up in the town of Triumph, not far from Sun Valley, Picabo Street (1971–) had plenty of opportunity to practice downhill skiing. When she was 17, she joined the U.S. Ski Team. She won a silver medal at the 1994 Olympics, and in the 1998 Olympics she carried away the gold. After the 2002 Olympics, she retired from competition. She was inducted into the National Ski Hall of Fame in 2005. Street's unusual first name (pronounced PEEK-a-boo) comes from a word that means "shining waters" in a Native American language.

? Want to know more? Visit www.factsfornow.scholastic.com and enter the keyword **Idaho**.

Harmon Killebrew

Idaho has no professional sports teams, but players from the Gem State have had outstanding careers on a number of pro teams. Harmon Killebrew of Payette hit 573 home runs during his long career in Major League Baseball. In 1984, he was elected to the National Baseball Hall of Fame. Vernon Law, who grew up in Meridian, pitched for the Pittsburgh Pirates for 16 years. Larry Jackson, a native of Nampa, pitched with the St. Louis Cardinals, the Chicago Cubs, and the Philadelphia Phillies. He returned to Idaho in 1970 and made a major career shift, spending eight years in the state legislature.

FAQ

Q8 WHERE DID THE UNIVERSITY OF IDAHO'S TEAM NICKNAME, THE VANDALS, COME FROM?

A8 The name comes from a warrior group called the Vandals, who wrecked the once-might Roman Empire. During the days of Coach Hec Edmundson, reporters were so impressed by the basketball team's defense they said the team "vandalized" their opponents. The university president went a step further and made Vandals the team's official nickname.

READ ABOUT

Governor Butch Otter addresses the Idaho state legislature in 2014.

CHAPTER SEVEN

GOVERNMENT

★

I N 2004, IDAHO FOURTH-GRADERS TOOK ACTION. Students from Meridian's Peregrine Elementary and Boise's St. Joseph's Elementary schools wrote to their state legislators and asked for the peregrine falcon to become Idaho's state raptor. Their idea was introduced to the legislature as House Bill 712. The bill passed in the house and the senate, and Governor Dirk Kempthorne signed it into law. These Idaho fourth-graders learned about the workings of government firsthand and saw how ordinary people can make things happen.

The state capitol in Boise

CAPITOL FACTS

Here are some fascinating facts about Idaho's state capitol:

- The present capitol was built with sandstone from a quarry on Table Rock east of Boise.
- Idaho's capitol is the only state capitol heated by **geothermal** water. A pump brings the hot water from 3,000 feet (914 m) underground.
- The eagle on the capitol dome is made of bronze-plated copper and stands 5 feet 7 inches (1.7 m) tall.
- A network of tunnels connects the capitol with the supreme court and other office buildings. Only government employees are allowed to use these tunnels.

WORD TO KNOW

geothermal *from underground hot springs*

GOVERNING IDAHO

Idaho's capital city, Boise, is the seat of state government. Under the 1890 state constitution, the government is divided into three branches: executive, legislative, and judicial.

EXECUTIVE BRANCH

The executive branch is headed by the governor, who is elected to a four-year term. The governor can serve an unlimited number of terms. The governor controls state spending and oversees the operation of state agencies. He or she also approves or vetoes (refuses to sign into law) bills that have been passed by the state legislature.

Voters also elect other top officials, including the lieutenant governor, who takes over if the governor can no longer serve; the secretary of state, who is in charge of state elections; the controller, who keeps track of the state's finances; the treasurer, who manages the state's money; the attorney general, who represents the state in legal cases; and the superintendent of public instruction, who heads the public school

Capital City

This map shows places of interest in Boise, Idaho's capital city.

MINI-BIO

MOSES ALEXANDER: FROM MEN'S SUITS TO THE GOVERNOR'S OFFICE

At age 14, Moses Alexander (1853–1932) emigrated from Germany to live with his older sister in New York. Later, he moved to Chillicothe, Missouri, where he started a clothing store. In the 1890s, there was a gold rush in Alaska, and Alexander caught gold fever. But when he passed through Idaho on his way north, he fell in love with the Gem State. He settled in Boise and opened a string of men's clothing stores. He also became Boise's mayor. In 1914 and again in 1916, Alexander was elected governor of Idaho.

❓ **Want to know more?** Visit www.factsfornow .scholastic.com and enter the keyword **Idaho**.

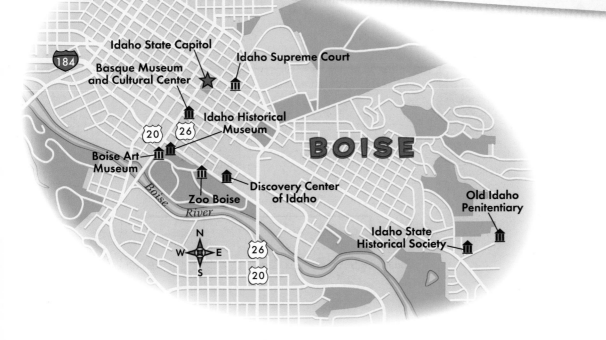

Idaho State Government

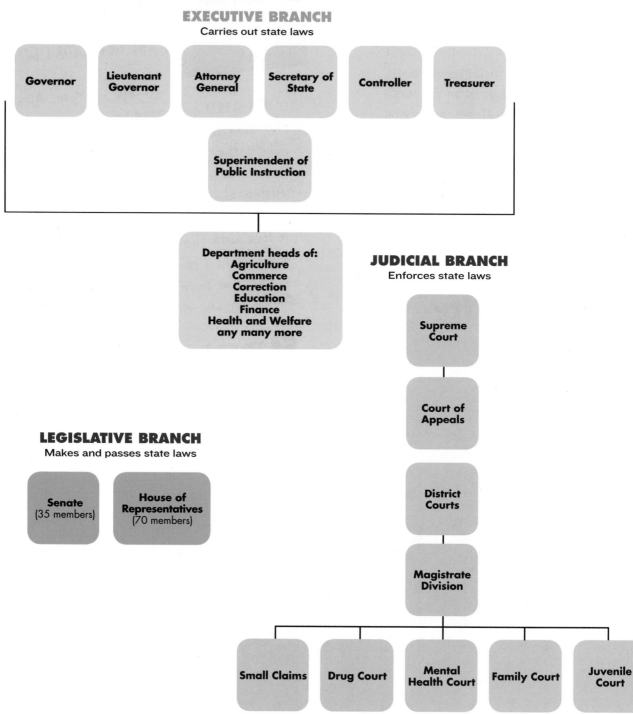

EXECUTIVE BRANCH
Carries out state laws

Governor

Lieutenant Governor

Attorney General

Secretary of State

Controller

Treasurer

Superintendent of Public Instruction

Department heads of:
Agriculture
Commerce
Correction
Education
Finance
Health and Welfare
any many more

JUDICIAL BRANCH
Enforces state laws

Supreme Court

Court of Appeals

District Courts

Magistrate Division

Small Claims

Drug Court

Mental Health Court

Family Court

Juvenile Court

LEGISLATIVE BRANCH
Makes and passes state laws

Senate
(35 members)

House of Representatives
(70 members)

system. All of these officials are elected to four-year terms.

LEGISLATIVE BRANCH

Idaho's legislature consists of two governing bodies: the house of representatives and the senate. Idaho has 35 legislative districts, and voters in each district elect two state representatives and one state senator. They all serve two-year terms.

Legislators discuss and vote on laws and budgets for the state. When both houses have passed a bill, or proposed law, it goes to the governor to be signed. The governor may either sign the bill, making it law, or veto it. If the governor vetoes a bill, it can still become law if enough legislators vote for it again.

JUDICIAL BRANCH

Each of Idaho's 44 counties has a magistrate who presides over local cases such as petty crimes and disputes between neighbors. More serious matters are sent to the district courts. Idaho has seven judicial districts. Voters in each district elect judges to serve four-year terms. From any of the district courts, a case can be sent to the court of **appeals**. The court of appeals has three judges elected to six-year terms.

The state supreme court is the highest court in Idaho. It hears cases that are

BUTCH OTTER: SERVING THE PEOPLE

Born in Caldwell, C. L. "Butch" Otter graduated from the College of Idaho in Boise in 1967 and served several years in the Idaho Army National Guard before embarking on a 30-year business career.

Otter was elected to the Idaho House of Representatives in 1972 and was reelected twice. From 1986 until 2000, he was the lieutenant governor of Idaho, and from 2000 to 2006, he served his home state in the U.S. House of Representatives. In 2006, he was elected governor of Idaho.

? **Want to know more?** Visit www.factsfornow .scholastic.com and enter the keyword **Idaho**.

Representing Idaho

This list shows the number of elected officials who represent Idaho, both on the state and national levels.

OFFICE	NUMBER	LENGTH OF TERM
State senators	35	2 years
State representatives	70	2 years
U.S. senators	2	6 years
U.S. representatives	2	2 years
Presidential electors	4	—

WORD TO KNOW

appeals *legal proceedings in which a court is asked to change the decision of a lower court*

appealed from the lower courts for a final decision. Idaho voters elect five judges to serve six-year terms on the supreme court. The members of the court choose one of their members to serve as chief justice. The other four supreme court judges are known as associate justices.

LOCAL GOVERNMENT

Each of Idaho's 44 counties is governed by a board with three, five, or seven commissioners. Two of the commissioners are elected to two-year terms, and one is elected to serve a four-year term. Most of Idaho's cities are governed by a mayor and city council.

MINI-BIO

FRANK CHURCH: GETTING A SECOND CHANCE

During law school, Frank Church (1924–1984) learned that he had cancer and had only a few months to live. Radiation treatment saved his life. Given a second chance, he vowed to make the most of it. Church was elected to four U.S. Senate terms, serving from 1957 to 1981. He sponsored the National Wilderness Act and the Wild and Scenic Rivers Act. He helped establish the Hells Canyon National Recreation Area on the Oregon-Idaho border. The Frank Church–River of No Return Wilderness was named in his honor in 1984, only a few weeks before cancer finally claimed his life.

? Want to know more? Visit www.factsfornow .scholastic.com and enter the keyword **Idaho**.

Idaho Counties

This map shows the **44** counties in Idaho.
Boise, the state capital, is indicated with a star.

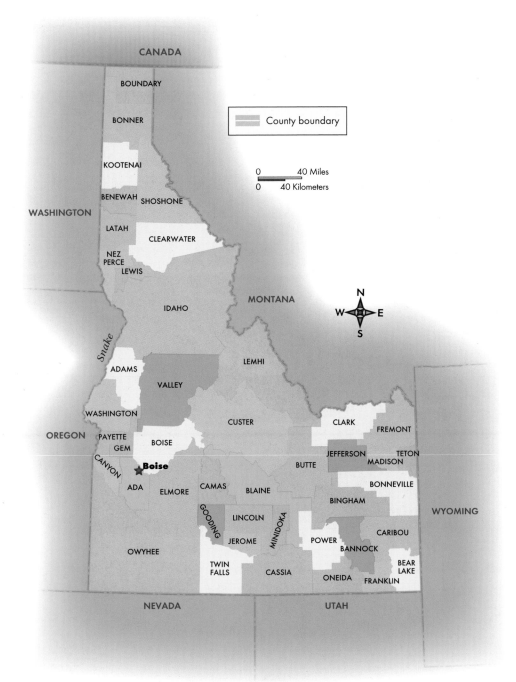

State Flag

The Idaho state flag has a blue background. The Idaho state seal is featured in the center of the flag, with a red banner underneath reading "State of Idaho." The flag was adopted in 1907.

State Seal

Idaho became a state on July 3, 1890. During that same summer, a young woman by the name of Emma Edwards visited Boise. She was invited to enter a design for the Great Seal of the State of Idaho contest. Upon winning the contest with her design, she became the first and only woman to design the great seal of a state. She later married, becoming Emma Edwards Green.

The seal features a miner on the right, which symbolizes the mining economy, and a woman on the left, with the state flower growing beside her, representing justice. Woman suffrage was a prominent issue at the time Edwards designed the seal, and she intentionally put the woman and man side by side as equals. The shield between them symbolizes protection. Inside the shield, the pine tree represents the timber industry and the farmer represents agriculture. The mighty Snake River runs down the center of the shield. The banner bears the state motto, *Esto Perpetua*, Latin for "Let It Be Perpetual."

98

READ ABOUT

An Idaho potato farmer checks his crops.

CHAPTER EIGHT

ECONOMY

★

AT A BIG FACTORY IN POCATELLO, WORKERS TURN OUT COMPUTER CHIPS. A lawyer in Twin Falls gives advice to a worried client. Dockworkers in Lewiston unload cargo from a giant steamship, and shearers harvest wool from sheep on a ranch in the Snake River Valley. All of these people are taking part in Idaho's economy. Service industries, manufacturing, agriculture, and mining all keep the Gem State's economy healthy.

ECONOMY ECONOMY ECONOMY ECONOMY ECONOMY ECONOM

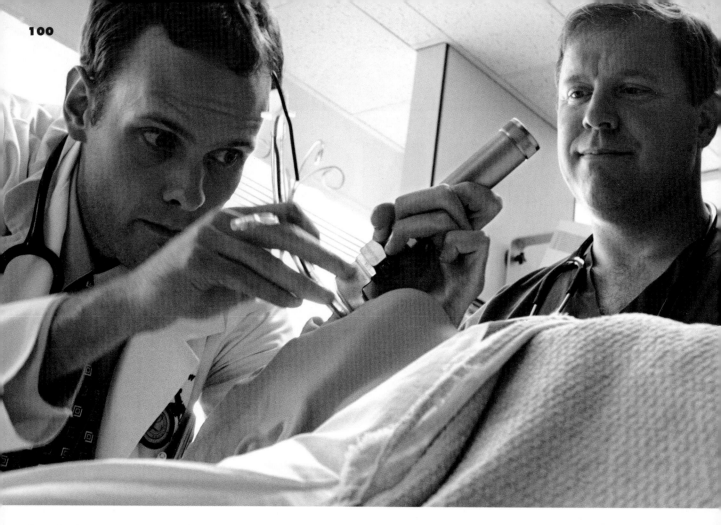

A medical student receives instruction in Boise.

WORD TO KNOW

gross state product *the total value of all the goods and services produced in a state*

On December 20, 1951, a power plant at what is now the Idaho National Laboratory successfully produced electricity from nuclear energy for the first time in history.

SERVICE INDUSTRIES

Idaho's service industries account for almost 80 percent of Idaho's **gross state product**. Service industries are industries in which people do things for others. Doctors, university professors, computer repair experts, and landscapers all work in service industries. The largest portion of Idaho's service industries is community, business, and personal services. Private health clinics, law firms, and repair shops all fall within this category. The second-largest portion of the service economy consists of real estate, insurance, and financial services. With several major banking headquarters, Boise is the state's leading financial center.

Restaurants, hotels, and commercial trade are all important elements in Idaho's service sector. These businesses are closely tied to tourism. Thousands of visitors pour into Idaho each year to enjoy the state's hunting, fishing, hiking, and skiing.

Workers in state and federal government make up the fourth-largest segment of the service economy in Idaho. Public school teachers and workers on Indian reservations are all government employees. So are guides in Idaho's state and national parks, and forest rangers in national forests.

MAKING THINGS FOR SALE

Computer-related materials are Idaho's leading manufactured product. ON Semiconductor makes microchips at a plant in Pocatello. The computer giant Hewlett-Packard turns out laser printers in Boise. Micron Technology, which is also located in Boise, designs and manufactures computer-memory products. The company employs roughly 5,600 Idahoans.

Food processing is another important part of the manufacturing sector in Idaho. Idaho plants pioneered the manufacture

MINI-BIO

JOSEPH ALBERTSON: FEEDING THE HUNGRY

As a young man, Joseph Albertson (1906–1993) took a job with the Safeway supermarket chain in Utah and spent 12 years learning the business. In 1939, he borrowed $5,000 and returned to Idaho to found the first Albertsons Supermarket in Boise. "In good times or bad people have to eat, so I figure it's a good business," he told an interviewer in 1969. Albertson's Boise store was the first in a chain that flourishes throughout the West today.

❓ **Want to know more?** Visit www.factsfornow.scholastic.com and enter the keyword **Idaho**.

SEE IT HERE!

IDAHO NATIONAL LABORATORY

In 1955, Arco, Idaho, made history when it became the first town in the world to be powered by atomic energy. That energy was produced by nuclear reactors at what is now known as the Idaho National Laboratory (INL). About 8,000 women and men work at the laboratory's three facilities in the desert between Arco and Idaho Falls. The INL is dedicated to developing nuclear power and finding effective ways to dispose of dangerous nuclear waste.

What Do Idahoans Do?

This color-coded chart shows what industries Idahoans work in.

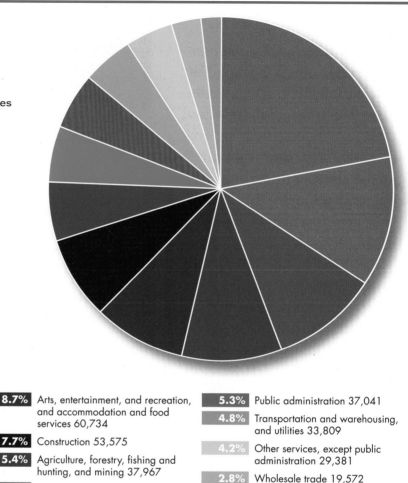

22.0%	Educational services, and health care and social assistance 153,985
12.3%	Retail trade 85,930
9.9%	Manufacturing 69,184
9.5%	Professional, scientific, and management, and administrative and waste management services 66,560
8.7%	Arts, entertainment, and recreation, and accommodation and food services 60,734
7.7%	Construction 53,575
5.4%	Agriculture, forestry, fishing and hunting, and mining 37,967
5.4%	Finance and insurance, and real estate and rental and leasing 37,435
5.3%	Public administration 37,041
4.8%	Transportation and warehousing, and utilities 33,809
4.2%	Other services, except public administration 29,381
2.8%	Wholesale trade 19,572
1.9%	Information 13,529

Source: U.S. Census Bureau, 2010 census

Nineteenth-century missionaries Henry and Eliza Spalding were the first people to plant potatoes in Idaho.

of frozen french fries, now a multimillion-dollar industry. Refineries in Idaho extract and purify sugar from sugar beets. Processed meats, canned fruits and vegetables, and dairy products are also produced in the state.

FROM THE LAND

When you mention Idaho to people outside the state, one word usually springs to mind: potatoes! The rich soil of the Snake River Valley is ideal for growing spuds. Idaho produces more potatoes than any other state in the nation.

Major Agricultural and Mining Products

This map shows where Idaho's major agricultural and mining products come from. See a cow? That means cattle are raised there.

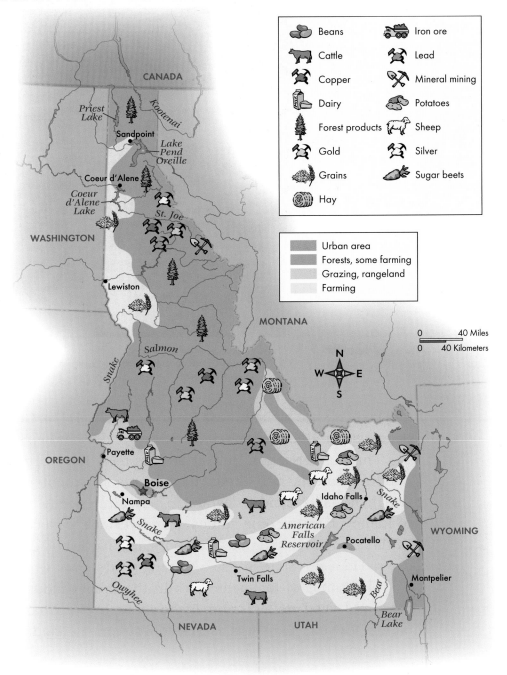

Legend:

- Beans
- Cattle
- Copper
- Dairy
- Forest products
- Gold
- Grains
- Hay
- Iron ore
- Lead
- Mineral mining
- Potatoes
- Sheep
- Silver
- Sugar beets

- Urban area
- Forests, some farming
- Grazing, rangeland
- Farming

0 — 40 Miles
0 — 40 Kilometers

CANADA

Priest Lake
Kootenai
Sandpoint
Lake Pend Oreille
Coeur d'Alene
Coeur d'Alene Lake
St. Joe
WASHINGTON
Lewiston
Salmon
Snake
MONTANA
OREGON
Payette
Boise
Nampa
Snake
American Falls Reservoir
Idaho Falls
Pocatello
Twin Falls
Owyhee
Bear
WYOMING
Montpelier
Bear Lake
NEVADA
UTAH

J. R. SIMPLOT: MR. SPUD

When John Richard (J. R.) Simplot (1909–2008) was only 14, he founded the J. R. Simplot Company and began packing and selling potatoes. He sensed that the nation's growing population needed easily prepared foods that could be stored for long periods. He learned everything he could about drying and freezing potatoes and other vegetables. Simplot branched into canned fruits and vegetables and developed frozen french fries. Though he became a billionaire, he claimed he was no genius. "I knew how to get a penny from a potato," he said in an interview, "and when I got that penny I saved it."

? Want to know more? Visit www.factsfornow.scholastic.com and enter the keyword **Idaho**.

Workers harvesting green peppers near New Plymouth

WOW

Idaho produces 12 billion pounds (5.4 billion kg) of potatoes each year.

Potatoes are by no means Idaho's only crop. The Gem State also produces wheat, hay, barley, and sugar beets.

Through irrigation, Idaho farmers have transformed parched deserts into productive farmland. About one-fourth of Idaho's land is devoted to agriculture today. Half of Idaho's farm income comes from livestock, especially cattle. Farmers in the state raise both beef cattle and dairy cows. The Gem State is also a leading producer of wool.

Thousands of Idahoans work in the timber industry. Wood and wood products from Idaho generate more than $2 billion per year. Timber is harvested from private land and from Idaho's national forests. Loggers cut Douglas fir, ponderosa pine, western larch, and many other trees.

Mining is one of Idaho's oldest industries, and it is still important today. Idaho quarries produce stone, sand, and gravel used in the construction business. Shoshone County in northern Idaho has several productive silver mines. Idaho is a leading producer of molybdenum, a mineral used in the process of making steel. Lovely gemstones called garnets are also found in the Gem State.

Top Products

Agriculture Dairy products, cattle and calves, potatoes, wheat, hay

Manufacturing Electrical equipment, food processing, lumber and wood, machinery, chemicals, printed materials

Mining Silver, phosphate rock (for fertilizer), gold, clays, copper, crushed stone, garnet, sand and gravel

The timber industry relies on trees like these in the Boise National Forest.

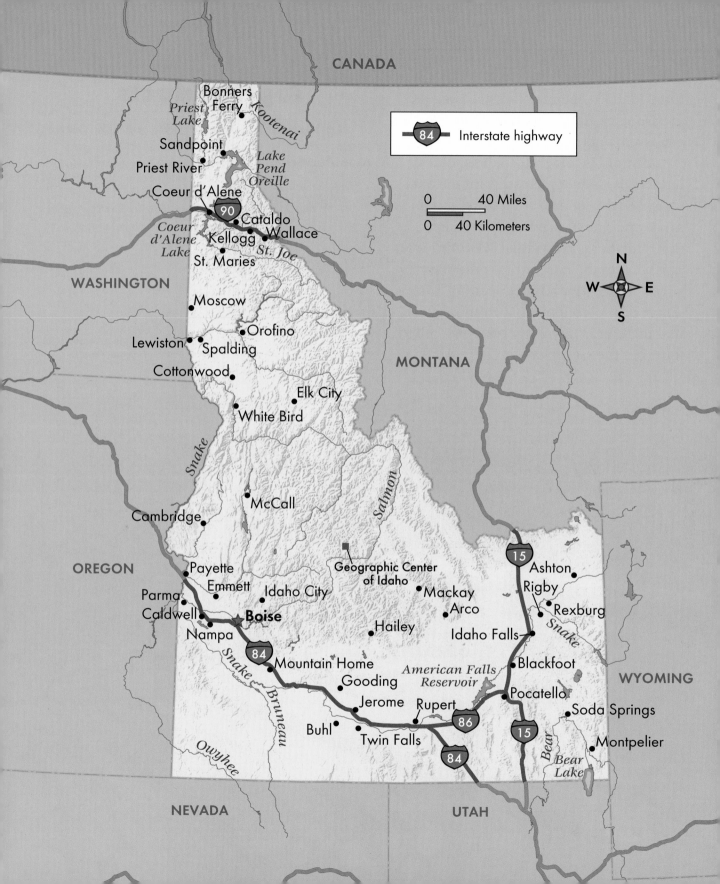

CHAPTER NINE

TRAVEL GUIDE

TRAVEL GUIDE

★

ARE YOU READY TO SEE IDAHO? From the rugged mountains of the Panhandle to the breathtaking splendor of Hells Canyon, from the High Desert to the streets of historic towns, the state's natural beauty and friendly people offer a bounty of gifts to the visitor. Hike its trails, view its lakes and mountains, and explore its many museums and historic sites.

← Follow along with this travel map. We'll begin in Bonners Ferry and end in Rigby!

NORTHERN IDAHO

THINGS TO DO: Test your daring on a roller coaster, pan for gold, and find out how many people it takes to encircle a giant tree.

Bonners Ferry

★ **Boundary County Museum:** The museum contains memorabilia from the days when a ferry carried passengers back and forth across the Kutenai River.

Coeur d'Alene

★ **Silverwood Theme Park:** Silverwood is the largest theme park in the Pacific Northwest. The Tremors roller coaster is a crazy ride through four wildly twisting underground tunnels. If that's not enough for you, hurtle 140 feet (43 m) from the top of the Panic Plunge drop tower!

The Tremors roller coaster at Silverwood Theme Park

Wallace

★ **Northern Pacific Railroad Depot Museum:** Housed in a historic train station, this museum focuses on the history of railroading in the Coeur d'Alene mining district. A prized display is a unique 13-foot (4 m) glass map of the Northern Pacific Railway.

★ **Hiawatha Trail:** Ten tunnels and seven trestle bridges remind hikers and bikers of the 15-mile (24 km) trail's history. It used to be a railroad track.

★ **Wallace District Mining Museum:** This museum traces the history of mining in northern Idaho from gold rush days to modern silver mining. View minerals and mining equipment, and see a video on mining history.

★ **Captain John Mullan Museum:** Through photos, newspaper clippings, early furniture, and vintage clothing, this museum takes visitors back to the late 19th century.

Kellogg

★ **Crystal Gold Mine:** This mine was worked between 1879 and 1881. Today, you can take a guided tour of the tunnels beneath the mountains. During the summer, you can try panning for gold.

Cataldo

★ **Old Mission State Park:** This 1853 mission church is the oldest building in Idaho. Walk through the Sacred Heart Mission headquarters, explore the historic cemetery, or see exhibits about local Indians and the mission's Jesuit founders.

Priest Lake

★ **Roosevelt Grove:** This is a virgin cedar forest, with some trees measuring 12 feet (3.7 m) in diameter and towering 150 feet (46 m) high. Scientists estimate that a few of them are as much as 3,000 years old!

Sandpoint

★ **Bonner County Historical Museum:** Among the displays at this museum are a pioneer kitchen, a vintage railroad caboose, and relics from the Farragut Naval Training Base.

NORTH CENTRAL IDAHO

THINGS TO DO: Take a trail ride on an Appaloosa, hike the rim of Hells Canyon, find out how young salmon are raised in fish hatcheries, and admire Nez Perce crafts.

Moscow

★ **Idaho Forest Fire Museum:** Exhibits at this museum explain how forest fires work within the natural cycle of destruction and renewal, and trace the history of firefighting in Idaho.

★ **Appaloosa Museum:** This museum celebrates the history of Idaho's state horse, the Appaloosa. See handmade saddles and bridles, learn about the role of the Appaloosa in Nez Perce culture, and take a trail ride to explore the surrounding countryside.

Appaloosa

IDAHO'S STATE HORSE

When Lewis and Clark reached Idaho in 1805, they noticed that the Nez Perce rode horses "of an excellent race; lofty, elegantly formed, active and durable." Some of these horses had black, white, and brown spots. The spotted horses came to be known as Palouses for the Palouse River. Eventually, they were called Appaloosas. Horse enthusiasts started to take an interest in the breed during the 1930s. In 1975, the Appaloosa became Idaho's official state horse.

Elk City

★ **Bitterroot National Forest:**
This 1.6-million-acre (640,000 ha) forest sprawls between Idaho and Montana. Half of the land is the largest roadless area in the continental United States!

Orofino

★ **Canoe Camp:** The Lewis and Clark expedition camped here in the autumn of 1805. See a replica of one of the five canoes they built with Nez Perce help for their journey down the Clearwater and Snake to the Columbia River.

★ **Clearwater Fish Hatchery:** Young fish are raised at this complex of hatcheries for release into the wild.

White Bird

★ **White Bird Battlefield:** The U.S. Army and Chief Joseph's Nez Perce Indians clashed here in 1877. Signs describe the battle and recount Chief Joseph's four-month flight from Oregon into Montana.

Spalding

★ **Nez Perce National Historical Park:** Artifacts and pictures reveal Nez Perce legends and history. Park rangers in traditional costume demonstrate Nez Perce crafts.

Cottonwood

★ **Historical Museum at St. Gertrude:** Some 60,000 artifacts from the region's history include minerals, firearms, and Nez Perce tools and weapons.

Lewiston

★ **Hells Canyon:** Explore one of the state's most spectacular sights in a boat, or hike or ride horseback along the rim. Indian rock paintings can be seen in caves and on the canyon walls.

Hells Canyon

SEE IT HERE!

CRATERS OF THE MOON NATIONAL MONUMENT AND PRESERVE

This 750,000-acre (303,500 ha) lava field may give you the feeling that you have left the planet Earth. In some places, lava seeped through cracks in the ground and cooled to form domes or shields. In other places, it spewed forth and formed towering cones. There are even tunnel-like caves called lava tubes.

SOUTH-WESTERN IDAHO

THINGS TO DO: Gaze up at strange rock formations, learn about the history of settlement in Idaho, and eat some Basque food.

Idaho City

★ **Boise Basin Museum:** This museum contains artifacts that recall the gold rush of the 1860s and the farming settlements that followed.

Boise

★ **Boise Art Museum:** Idaho's leading art museum contains an important collection of art by Idaho artists.

★ **Boise Depot:** This handsome building was built in 1925 as a station for the Union Pacific Railroad. Today, the eight-story waiting room is used for special events and concerts.

★ **Idaho Historical Museum:** Get an overview of Idaho history, from ancient people to modern agriculture and industry.

★ **Discovery Center of Idaho:** This science museum has more than 130 hands-on exhibits that challenge your powers of reason.

★ **Basque Museum and Cultural Center:** Learn about Basque music, dance, and food. And discover how Basque shepherds helped settle the West.

★ **Old Idaho Penitentiary:** Built in 1872, this prison was once the home of some of the toughest criminals in the West. Tour the cell blocks, and then visit the site's collection of Revolutionary War and Civil War artifacts.

★ **Boise State University Vertebrate Museum:** See an amazing collection of stuffed mammals, birds, reptiles, amphibians, and fish, especially species found in the Boise area.

Melba

★ **Celebration Park:** Guided walking tours of Idaho's only archaeological park explain the rock carvings made by Native peoples more than 12,000 years ago.

Nampa

★ **Warhawk Air Museum:** This museum features U.S. and foreign aircraft from World War I to the Vietnam War. Weather permitting, the museum puts on air shows with some of these classic planes.

Shoshone Falls

Cambridge

★ **Cambridge Museum:** Exhibits on local history include displays of rocks and minerals, Native American tools and jewelry, and early farming equipment.

Jerome

★ **Minidoka National Historic Site:** Walk among the ruins of the camp buildings and try to imagine life behind the barbed wire for some 13,000 Japanese Americans during World War II.

Twin Falls

★ **Herrett Center for Arts and Science:** From a Latin American art collection to painting and sculpture by today's Idaho and Pacific Northwest artists, the center exhibits a wide range of artwork. It also includes the Faulkner Planetarium.

Shoshone Falls is a waterfall on the Snake River in southern Idaho. Often called the Niagara of the West, it is 212 feet (65 m) high—45 feet (14 m) taller than Niagara Falls itself!

Malta

★ **City of Rocks National Reserve:**
The wind has carved cones of
volcanic rock into a series of strange
towers. Adding to the unearthly
quality of the place, the rocks are
sometimes covered with bright
green lichens.

SOUTH-EASTERN IDAHO

**THING TO DO: Explore a
replica of Old Fort Hall, see the world's biggest
potato chip, and visit the world's only human-
made geyser.**

Pocatello

★ **Bannock County Historical
Museum:** Learn local history
through artifacts of the Bannock
and Shoshone peoples and through
memorabilia from Pocatello's early
railroads.

★ **Fort Hall Replica:** Enter the heavy
wooden gates to explore the black-
smith shop, carpenter's quarters,
Indian trading post, and other buildings. Outside the fort, climb aboard a
covered wagon or step inside a tepee.

★ **Idaho Museum of Natural
History:** Dinosaur skeletons, exhibits on volcanoes and glaciers, and
displays of edible plants tell Idaho's
natural history.

Blackfoot

★ **Bingham County Historical
Museum:** Housed in a 15-room
mansion, this museum contains
a collection of antique dolls and
Native American artifacts.

★ **Idaho Potato Museum:** Watch a
video on the history of the potato
industry, visit exhibits on the potato
in ancient agriculture, and see the
world's biggest potato chip!

Soda Springs

★ **Soda Springs Geyser:**
An accident created
this geyser in 1937
when workers drilling
a well hit a natural
spring. Spouts of
water shoot 70 feet
(21 m) into the air
every hour through-
out the day.

Soda Springs Geyser

EASTERN IDAHO

THINGS TO DO: Explore the highest spot in Idaho, see the world's first television tube, and watch a video of the Teton Dam collapsing in 1976.

Idaho Falls

★ **Museum of Idaho:** National exhibits on history and the sciences stop here when they are on tour.

★ **Willard Arts Center:** Works by internationally recognized artists and local painters and sculptors grace the galleries, including a room devoted to art by local children.

★ **Tautphaus Park Zoo:** With more than 400 species, this zoo features the largest collection of animals in the state of Idaho. Visit the Children's Zoo to enjoy a hands-on experience with incredible wildlife!

Arco

★ **Natural Bridge:** Carved by wind and rain, this huge arch stands 80 feet (24 m) high and is one of Idaho's extraordinary natural features.

Mackay

★ **Moose Center Learning Lab:** Everything you ever wanted to know about the North American moose is gathered here under one roof! Pore over photos and scientific articles. Listen to recorded moose calls, and try imitating the sounds you hear.

★ **Borah Peak:** Snowcapped Borah Peak is the highest spot in Idaho. At its base, you can see the crack left by Idaho's biggest earthquake.

★ **Lost River Museum:** Built in a 100-year-old church, this museum is filled with artifacts and information about the history of the area, from railroads to clothing styles.

Borah Peak

MINI-BIO

PHILO T. FARNSWORTH: TEENAGE GENIUS

When radio stations began to broadcast in 1921, most Americans were dazzled. But 15-year-old Philo T. Farnsworth (1906–1971) wanted more. He thought there had to be a way to add pictures to the sound. As a project for his science class at Rigby High School, he designed a television. During his lifetime, Farnsworth **patented** 160 parts for the television and radio.

? **Want to know more?** Visit www.factsfornow .scholastic.com and enter the keyword **Idaho**.

National Oregon/California Trail Center

Montpelier

★ **National Oregon/California Trail Center:** Guides in period costume take the whole family on a simulated trip along the Oregon Trail, bringing the experience to life.

Rexburg

★ **Legacy Flight Museum:** This museum preserves the history of U.S. military aircraft. Retired planes from World War II and other conflicts are on display.

★ **Teton Flood Museum:** Photos and newspaper clippings tell the sobering story of the 1976 flood and its aftermath. Watch a video of the dam breaking, and tour the disaster site.

WORD TO KNOW

patented *received the right to make or use an invention for a certain number of years*

Rigby

★ **Farnsworth TV and Pioneer Museum:** The museum displays the first television tube, invented here by Philo T. Farnsworth, along with Indian artifacts and the mounted heads of deer, elk, and bighorn sheep.

WRITING PROJECTS

Check out these ideas for creating a campaign brochure and writing you-are-there narratives. Or research the lives of famous Idahoans.

118

ART PROJECTS

You can illustrate the state song, create a dazzling PowerPoint presentation, or learn about the state quarter and design your own.

119

IDAHO 1890
ESTO PERPETUA
2007
E PLURIBUS UNUM

TIMELINE

What happened when? This timeline highlights important events in the state's history—and shows what was happening throughout the United States at the same time.

122

FAST FACTS

Use this section to find fascinating facts about state symbols, land area and population statistics, weather, sports teams, and much more.

126

GLOSSARY

Remember the Words to Know from the chapters in this book? They're all collected here.

125

SCIENCE, TECHNOLOGY, ENGINEERING, & MATH PROJECTS

120

Make weather maps, graph population statistics, and research endangered species that live in the state.

PRIMARY VS. SECONDARY SOURCES

121

So what are primary and secondary sources? And what's the diff? This section explains all that and where you can find them.

BIOGRAPHICAL DICTIONARY

133

This at-a-glance guide highlights some of the state's most important and influential people. Visit this section and read about their contributions to the state, the country, and the world.

RESOURCES

Books and much more. Take a look at these additional sources for information about the state.

138

WRITING PROJECTS

Write a Memoir, Journal Entry, or Editorial for Your School Newspaper!

Picture Yourself . . .

★ At a Paiute festival. Describe the sights, sounds, and smells of the gathering. What games do people play? What are some of the other activities they take part in?

SEE: Chapter Two, page 31.

★ With your family on the Oregon Trail heading west through Idaho. What hardships would you endure along the way? What kind of adventures would you have?

SEE: Chapter Three, pages 44–45.

Create an Election Brochure or Web Site!

Run for office! Throughout this book, you've read about some of the issues that concern Idaho today. As a candidate for governor of Idaho, create a campaign brochure or Web site.

★ Explain how you meet the qualifications to be governor of Idaho.

★ Talk about the three or four major issues you'll focus on if you're elected.

★ Remember, you'll be responsible for Idaho's budget. How would you spend the taxpayers' money?

SEE: Chapter Seven, pages 90–92.

Create an Interview Script with a Famous Person from Idaho!

★ Research various Idahoans, such as Sacagawea, Edward Pulaski, Barbara Morgan, Picabo Street, J. R. Simplot, or Philo T. Farnsworth.

★ Based on your research, pick one person you would most like to talk with.

★ Write a script of the interview. What questions would you ask? How would this person answer? Create a question-and-answer format. You may want to supplement this writing project with a voice-recording dramatization of the interview.

SEE: Chapters Three, Five, Six, Eight, and Nine, pages 35, 63, 71, 87, 104, 115, and the Biographical Dictionary, pages 133–137.

ART PROJECTS

Create a PowerPoint Presentation or Visitors' Guide

Welcome to Idaho!

Idaho is a great place to visit and to live! From its natural beauty to its bustling cities and historical sites, there's plenty to see and do. In your PowerPoint presentation or brochure, highlight 10 to 15 of Idaho's interesting landmarks. Be sure to include:

★ a map of the state showing where these sites are located

★ photos, illustrations, Web links, natural history facts, geographic stats, climate and weather info, and descriptions of plants and wildlife

> **SEE:** Chapter Nine, pages 106–115, and Fast Facts, pages 126–127.

Illustrate the Lyrics to the Idaho State Song
("Here We Have Idaho")

Use markers, paints, photos, collages, colored pencils, or computer graphics to illustrate the lyrics to "Here We Have Idaho." Turn your illustrations into a picture book, or scan them into PowerPoint and add music.

SEE: The lyrics to "Here We Have Idaho" on page 128.

Research Idaho's State Quarter

From 1999 to 2008, the U.S. Mint introduced new quarters commemorating each of the 50 states in the order that they were admitted to the Union. Each state's quarter features a unique design on its reverse, or back.

★ Research the significance of the image. Who designed the quarter? Who chose the final design?

★ Design your own Idaho quarter. What images would you choose for the reverse?

★ Make a poster showing the Idaho quarter and label each image.

GO TO: www.factsfornow.scholastic.com. Enter the keyword **Idaho** and look for the link to the Idaho quarter.

SCIENCE, TECHNOLOGY, ENGINEERING, & MATH PROJECTS

Graph Population Statistics!

★ Compare population statistics (such as ethnic background, birth, death, and literacy rates) in Idaho counties or major cities.

★ In your graph or chart, look at population density and write sentences describing what the population statistics show; graph one set of population statistics and write a paragraph explaining what the graphs reveal.

SEE: Chapter Six, pages 74–77.

Create a Weather Map of Idaho!

Use your knowledge of Idaho's geography to research and identify conditions that result in specific weather events. What is it about the geography of Idaho that makes it vulnerable to things such as scorching heat and heavy snowfall? Create a weather map or poster that shows the weather patterns over the state. Include a caption explaining the technology used to measure weather phenomena and provide data.

SEE: Chapter One, pages 16–17.

Sockeye salmon

Track Endangered Species

Using your knowledge of Idaho's wildlife, research which animals and plants are endangered or threatened.

★ Find out what the state is doing to protect these species.

★ Chart known populations of the animals and plants, and report on changes in certain geographic areas.

SEE: Chapter One, pages 19–20.

PRIMARY VS. SECONDARY SOURCES

What's the Diff?

Your teacher may require at least one or two primary sources and one or two secondary sources for your assignment. So, what's the difference between the two?

★ **Primary sources are original.** You are reading the actual words of someone's diary, journal, letter, autobiography, or interview. Primary sources can also be photographs, maps, prints, cartoons, news/film footage, posters, first-person newspaper articles, drawings, musical scores, and recordings. By the way, when you conduct a survey, interview someone, shoot a video, or take photographs to include in a project, you are creating primary sources!

★ **Secondary sources are what you find in encyclopedias, textbooks, articles, biographies, and almanacs.** These are written by a person or group of people who tell about something that happened to someone else. Secondary sources also recount what another person said or did. This book is an example of a secondary source.

Now that you know what primary sources are—where can you find them?

★ **Your school or local library:** Check the library catalog for collections of original writings, government documents, musical scores, and so on. Some of this material may be stored on microfilm.

★ **Historical societies:** These organizations keep historical documents, photographs, and other materials. Staff members can help you find what you are looking for. History museums are also great places to see primary sources firsthand.

★ **The Internet:** There are lots of sites that have primary sources you can download and use in a project or assignment.

TIMELINE

★ ★ ★

U.S. Events

	Idaho Events

c. 5500 BCE

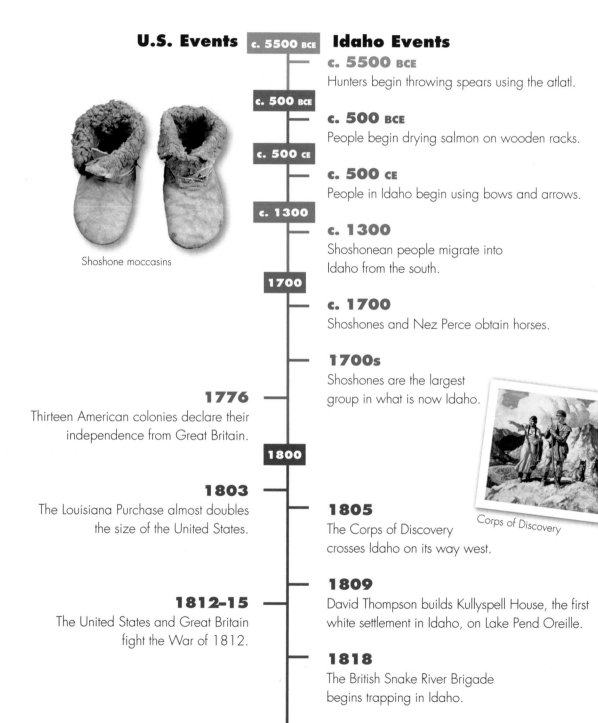

c. 5500 BCE
Hunters begin throwing spears using the atlatl.

c. 500 BCE

c. 500 BCE
People begin drying salmon on wooden racks.

c. 500 CE

c. 500 CE
People in Idaho begin using bows and arrows.

c. 1300

c. 1300
Shoshonean people migrate into Idaho from the south.

Shoshone moccasins

1700

c. 1700
Shoshones and Nez Perce obtain horses.

1700s
Shoshones are the largest group in what is now Idaho.

1776
Thirteen American colonies declare their independence from Great Britain.

Corps of Discovery

1800

1803
The Louisiana Purchase almost doubles the size of the United States.

1805
The Corps of Discovery crosses Idaho on its way west.

1809
David Thompson builds Kullyspell House, the first white settlement in Idaho, on Lake Pend Oreille.

1812–15
The United States and Great Britain fight the War of 1812.

1818
The British Snake River Brigade begins trapping in Idaho.

U.S. Events

Idaho Events

1822
William Henry Ashley sends American trappers into the Rockies.

1830
The Indian Removal Act forces eastern Native American groups to relocate west of the Mississippi River.

1836
Henry and Eliza Spalding establish a mission among the Nez Perce at Lapwai.

1840s
Thousands of settlers pass through Idaho on the Oregon Trail.

1846–48
The United States fights a war with Mexico over western territories in the Mexican War.

1846
Great Britain and the United States sign a treaty establishing a boundary between British and U.S. territory in the Northwest.

1855
A group of Mormon settlers establish Fort Lemhi on the Lemhi River.

1860
Elias Davidson Pierce finds gold in Orofino Creek.

1861–65
The American Civil War is fought between the Northern Union and the Southern Confederacy; it ends with the surrender of the Confederate army, led by General Robert E. Lee.

1863
President Abraham Lincoln issues the Emancipation Proclamation.

1863
Idaho becomes a U.S. territory; U.S. troops massacre hundreds of Shoshones at Bear River.

1877
Chief Joseph leads the Oregon band of Nez Perce across Idaho in an effort to escape forced removal to a reservation.

1890
Idaho becomes the 43rd state.

Chief Joseph

U.S. Events

Idaho Events

1896
Women in Idaho win the right to vote.

1899
Governor Frank Steunenberg calls in troops to end violent protests at mines.

1900

1910
The "Big Burn" destroys 3 million acres (1.2 million ha) of forest in northern Idaho.

1917–18
The United States engages in World War I.

1929
The stock market crashes, plunging the United States more deeply into the Great Depression.

1941–45
The United States engages in World War II.

1942–45
Japanese Americans are held prisoner at Minidoka detention camp.

1949
The U.S. government opens the Idaho National Engineering Laboratory near Arco.

1950–53
The United States engages in the Korean War.

1964–73
The United States engages in the Vietnam War.

1976
The Teton Dam collapses.

1991
The United States and other nations engage in the brief Persian Gulf War against Iraq.

1990–2006
Idaho's Latino population more than doubles.

2000

2001
Terrorists attack the United States on September 11.

2003
The United States and coalition forces invade Iraq.

2008
The United States elects its first African American president, Barack Obama.

2013
Wildfires rage in southern and southwestern Idaho.

GLOSSARY

★ ★ ★

appeals legal proceedings in which a court is asked to change the decision of a lower court

aquifer an underground layer of soil or loose rock that holds water

breechcloth a garment worn by a man over his lower body

convert to bring (a person) over from one opinion or belief to another

foreclosure a legal process for taking back property when the payment for it is overdue

geologists scientists who study the history of Earth

geothermal from underground hot springs

gross state product the total value of all the goods and services produced in a state

irrigation watering land by artificial means to promote plant growth

magnate a person with money and power, especially someone in industry

martial law law carried out by military forces

missionaries people who try to convert others to a religion

parallel a horizontal line on a map or globe; a line of latitude

patented received the right to make or use an invention for a certain number of years

philanthropist a person who helps others by giving time and money to causes and charities

porous capable of absorbing liquids

precipitation all water that falls to the earth, including rain, sleet, hail, snow, dew, fog, or mist

stockade a fort built with walls of poles driven into the ground

suffrage the right to vote

tectonic describing the structure of the earth's outer layer

vigilantes volunteers who decide on their own to stop crime and punish suspected criminals

FAST FACTS

★ ★ ★

State Symbols

Statehood date	July 3, 1890, the 43rd state
Origin of state name	An invented "Indian" word that is supposed to mean "gem of the mountains"
State capital	Boise
State nickname	Gem State
State motto	*Esto Perpetua* ("Let It Be Perpetual")
State bird	Mountain bluebird
State flower	Syringa
State fish	Cutthroat trout
State gem	Star garnet
State song	"Here We Have Idaho"
State tree	Western white pine
State fairs	Boise in late August and Blackfoot in early September

State seal

Geography

Total area; rank	83,568 square miles (216,442 sq km); 14th
Land; rank	82,643 square miles (214,045 sq km); 11th
Water; rank	926 square miles (2,398 sq km); 33rd
Inland water; rank	926 square miles (2,398 sq km); 25th
Geographic center	Custer County, southwest of Challis
Latitude	42° N to 49° N
Longitude	111° W to 117° W
Highest point	Borah Peak, 12,662 feet (3,859 m) in Custer County
Lowest point	710 feet (216 m) along the Snake River in Nez Perce County
Largest city	Boise
Longest river	Snake River
Number of counties	44

Population

Population; rank (2010 census)	1,567,582; 39th
Density (2010 census)	19 persons per square mile (7 per sq km)
Population distribution (2010 census)	71% urban, 21% rural
Ethnic distribution (2010 census)	White persons: 84.0%
	Persons of Hispanic or Latino origin: 11.2%
	Persons reporting two or more races: 1.7%
	Asian persons: 1.2%
	American Indian and Alaska Native persons: 1.1%
	Black persons: 0.6%
	Native Hawaiian and other Pacific Islanders: 0.1%
	Persons of another race: 0.1%

Weather

Record high temperature	118°F (48°C) at Orofino on July 28, 1934
Record low temperature	–60°F (–51°C) at Island Park Dam on January 18, 1943
Average July temperature, Boise	75°F (24°C)
Average January temperature, Boise	32°F (0°C)
Average yearly precipitation, Boise	12 inches (30 cm)

State flag

STATE SONG

★ ★ ★

"Here We Have Idaho"

The song, originally called "Garden of Paradise," was part of a contest. McKinley Helm, a University of Idaho student, wrote a verse to "Garden of Paradise" and won first place. He called the song "Our Idaho," and it became the school song. In 1931, the title was changed again to "Here We Have Idaho," after it was chosen as the state song by the Idaho legislature. Albert J. Tompkins wrote additional words, and Sallie Hume-Douglas wrote the music.

And here we have Idaho
Winning her way to fame.
Silver and gold in the sunlight blaze,
And romance lies in her name.

Singing, we're singing of you,
Ah, proudly, too; all our lives through,
We'll go singing,
Singing of you,
Singing of Idaho.

There's truly one state in this great land of ours,
Where ideals can be realized.
The pioneers made it so for you and me,
A legacy we'll always prize.

NATURAL AREAS AND HISTORIC SITES

National Park

Yellowstone National Park, which is bursting with geysers and hot springs, is the oldest national park in the world.

National Reserve

City of Rocks National Reserve is a landmark featuring wagon ruts and axle grease signatures left by emigrants heading west on the California Trail. The reserve also includes granite pinnacles more than 60 stories tall and 2.5 billion years old.

National Monuments

Craters of the Moon National Monument and Preserve features an otherworldly landscape created by lava eruptions.

Hagerman Fossil Beds National Monument features fossils from more than 200 species of plants and animals.

Minidoka National Historic Site commemorates the internment, hardships, and sacrifices of about 10,000 Japanese Americans during World War II.

National Historical Park

The *Nez Perce National Historical Park*, which lies in Idaho and within three other states, commemorates the stories and history of the Nimi'ipuu people.

National Historic Trails

Four national historic trails cross through Idaho: the *California National Historic Trail*, and the *Oregon National Historic Trail*, which follow the routes west taken by pioneers and gold miners seeking new opportunities; the *Lewis & Clark National Historic Trail*, which follows the trail of Lewis and Clark's journey; and the *Nez Perce (Nee Me Poo) National Historic Trail*, which follows the route Nez Perce people used to escape from the U.S. military into Canada.

National Forests

Idaho has 10 national forests and one national grassland.

State Parks

Idaho's state park system features and maintains 27 state parks, which include the beautiful *Trail of the Coeur d'Alenes* and the *Bear Lake State Park*.

SPORTS TEAMS

★ ★ ★

NCAA Teams (Division I)

Boise State University *Broncos*
Idaho State University *Bengals*
University of Idaho *Vandals*

Boise State taking on Idaho State in 2002

CULTURAL INSTITUTIONS

★ ★ ★

Libraries

The *Boise Public Library* is Idaho's largest public library.

The *Idaho Historical Museum* (Boise) houses many historical manuscripts and newspapers. It is also the official depository for state records.

The *Idaho State Law Library*, which was founded in 1869, houses Idaho's largest legal collection.

Museums

The *Basque Museum and Cultural Center* (Boise) has exhibits and events about Idaho's Basque community, people whose ancestors came from the mountains between Spain and France.

The *Boise Art Museum* is the largest art museum in Idaho. It has a fine collection of Pacific Northwest art and ceramics as well as art from around the world.

The *Idaho Black History Museum* (Boise) explores the experiences of African Americans in Idaho.

The *Idaho Museum of Mining and Geology* (Boise) displays rocks, fossils, and mining exhibits.

The *Idaho Historical Museum* (Boise) is Idaho's largest and most visited museum. Its exhibits bring to life Idaho's past, from the lives of Native Americans hundreds of years ago through the fur trade, pioneer times, and much more.

The *Idaho Museum of Natural History* (Pocatello) has exhibits on dinosaurs, volcanoes, regional plants and animals, and much more.

Performing Arts

The *Boise Philharmonic*, established in 1960, performs classical and new works in auditoriums and schools throughout Idaho.

Opera Idaho (Boise) produces classic grand opera and musical comedy shows, and features a Children's Chorus, founded in 1993.

Universities and Colleges

In 2011, Idaho had four public and seven private institutions of higher learning.

ANNUAL EVENTS

January–March
Sun Valley Winter Wonderland Festival (January)

Winter Sports Carnival in McCall (January)

Lionel Hampton International Jazz Festival in Moscow (February)

April–June
Dogwood Festival in Lewiston (April)

Cinco de Mayo Festival in Boise (May)

Moscow Renaissance Fair in Moscow (May)

Annual Bigwater Blowout in Riggins (June)

National Oldtime Fiddlers' Contest in Weiser (June)

July–September
Julyamsh Powwow in Post Falls (July)

Snake River Stampede Rodeo in Nampa (July)

Diamond Cup hydroplane races at Coeur d'Alene Lake (late July/early August)

Raspberry Festival in Cottonwood (August)

Western Idaho State Fair in Boise (August)

Eastern Idaho State Fair in Blackfoot (August–September)

Lewiston Roundup in Lewiston (September)

Lumberjack Days in Orofino (September)

October–December
Trailing of the Sheep Festival in Sun Valley (October)

Yuletide Lighting Festival in Wallace (December)

Western Idaho State Fair

BIOGRAPHICAL DICTIONARY

Joseph Albertson See page 101.

Moses Alexander See page 91.

Cecil D. Andrus See page 20.

Vernon Baker See page 66.

Glenn Balch (1902–1989) wrote numerous novels for young readers. Most of his books are about horses and take place in Idaho's Sawtooth Mountains.

Kim Barnes (1958–) is an essayist and poet who grew up in the logging country around Lewiston. She has written about her early life in books such as *In the Wilderness: Coming of Age in Unknown Country* and *Hungry for the World*.

T. H. Bell (1921–1996), born in Lava Hot Springs, was the U.S. secretary of education from 1981 to 1985. A former high school teacher and college professor, he worked to improve educational standards in the United States.

Polly Bemis See page 51.

Ezra Taft Benson (1899–1994), who was born in Whitney, served as U.S. secretary of agriculture for eight years under President Dwight D. Eisenhower. He also headed the Church of Jesus Christ of Latter-day Saints from 1985 until his death.

Gutzon Borglum (1867–1941), who was born John Gutzon de la Mothe Borglum, was a sculptor best known for carving the faces of four U.S. presidents on Mount Rushmore in South Dakota. He was born in a cabin on Bear Lake.

Gregory "Pappy" Boyington (1912–1988) was a U.S. Marine fighter pilot ace during World War II who was awarded both the Medal of Honor and the Navy Cross. A native of Coeur d'Alene, he commanded a group of fliers known as the Black Sheep Squadron, which inspired the 1970s hit TV show *Baa Baa Black Sheep*.

Jim Bridger (1804–1881) was a mountain man who explored Idaho and led expeditions throughout the Rocky Mountain region.

Carol Ryrie Brink See page 81.

Mary T. Brooks (1907–2002), who grew up in Gooding, served as director of the U.S. Mint from 1969 to 1977.

Margaretta Favorite Brown (1818–1897) was a painter who captured scenes of Idaho's mining camps in the 1860s and 1870s.

Frank Church See page 94.

Lou Dobbs (1945–), who grew up in Rupert, is a political and economic commentator on radio and television, and the host of TV's *Lou Dobbs Tonight* show.

Ezra Taft Benson

Stacy Dragila

Stacy Dragila (1971–) of Pocatello won the first-ever Olympic gold medal in women's pole vaulting in 2000. She has set many world records and coaches at Rocky Mountain High School in Meridian.

Fred T. Dubois See page 57.

Abigail Scott Duniway See page 62.

Bill Fagerbakke (1957–), who graduated from the University of Idaho, played the assistant coach, Dauber, on the TV series *Coach*. He is also the voice of SpongeBob SquarePants's friend Patrick.

Bill Fagerbakke

Philo T. Farnsworth See page 115.

Vardis Fisher (1895–1968), who was born in Annis, wrote numerous novels about pioneer life in Idaho, including *Children of God* about an early Mormon community.

Mary Hallock Foote (1847–1938) settled on the Idaho frontier as a young woman. She wrote and illustrated numerous books about Idaho life, including *Edith Bonham*, a novel based on her own experiences.

Gretchen Fraser (1919–1994), a longtime resident of Sun Valley, was the first American to win an Olympic gold medal in skiing. At the 1948 Winter Olympics in St. Moritz, Switzerland, she won the slalom event, as well as a silver medal in a slalom-downhill combined event.

Gretchen Fraser

John C. Frémont (1813–1890) was an explorer and soldier. He led a series of expeditions across the Rocky Mountain region during the 1840s and explored the Snake River Valley.

Emma Edwards Green (1856–1942) was an artist who designed Idaho's state seal. She was the first woman ever to design the seal of a U.S. state.

Janet Campbell Hale (1947–) is a writer who lived for a time on the Coeur d'Alene reservation in Idaho. Her book *The Owl's Song* looks at racial prejudice, and *Bloodlines* is her autobiography.

William Averell Harriman

William Averell Harriman (1891–1986) was a statesman and businessman. In 1936, he founded Sun Valley, the first U.S. ski resort. He served as U.S. ambassador to the Soviet Union (1943–46), U.S. secretary of commerce (1946–48), and governor of New York (1955–58). Under presidents John F. Kennedy and Lyndon B. Johnson, he was active in negotiating foreign affairs.

Gene Harris (1933–2000) was a jazz pianist who lived in Boise for a time. Boise's annual Gene Harris Jazz Festival has been held in his honor since 1998.

Ernest Hemingway (1899–1961) was one of the greatest writers of the 20th century and was awarded the 1954 Nobel Prize in Literature. His spare, powerful books include *The Sun Also Rises* and *The Old Man and the Sea*. He wrote his masterpiece *For Whom the Bell Tolls* at the Sun Valley Lodge near Ketchum, where he lived for many years.

May Arkwright Hutton See page 61.

Harmon Killebrew (1936–2011), a baseball player born in Payette, hit 573 home runs during his professional career. He played with the Washington Senators, the Minnesota Twins, and the Kansas City Royals. He was inducted into the National Baseball Hall of Fame in 1984.

Jerry Kramer (1936–), a resident of Sandpoint and a graduate of the University of Idaho, was a football player who spent 11 years with the Green Bay Packers (1958–1968). During that time, the Packers won five championships and the first two Super Bowls ever played.

Alex Kuo (1939–) is a poet and novelist who taught at the University of Idaho at Moscow. *Lipstick and Other Stories* (2002) won the American Book Award of the Before Columbus Foundation.

Mark Lindsay See page 85.

William McConnell (1839–1925) served as governor of Idaho from 1893 to 1897. He fought for better irrigation laws and helped women gain the right to vote.

Barbara Morgan See page 71.

Mourning Dove (1888–1936), who was born in a canoe on the Kutenai River, is considered the first female Native American novelist. *Cogewea, the Half-Blood*, was published in 1928.

Dan O'Brien (1966–), who won the gold medal for the decathlon at the 1996 Olympics, has been called the world's greatest living athlete. He attended the University of Idaho, and the university's Dan O'Brien Track and Field Complex is named in his honor.

Dan O'Brien

Charles Ostner (1828–1913) was a sculptor who ran a ferry on the Payette River. His life-sized wood carving of George Washington on a horse stands in the Idaho state capitol.

Butch Otter See page 93.

Aaron Paul (1979–) is an actor who was born in Emmett and grew up in Boise. He has been acclaimed for his work on television series such as *Big Love* and *Breaking Bad*. Paul has been nominated for five Emmy Awards and won two.

Gracie Bowers Pfost (1906–1965) was the first woman to represent Idaho in the U.S. Congress. She served from 1953 to 1963.

Elias Davidson Pierce (1824–1897) was a gold seeker who found gold in Orofino Creek in 1860.

Pocatello (1815–1884) was a leader of the Shoshone Nation. During the 1850s, he led a series of raids on wagon trains along the Oregon Trail in Idaho. After the Bear River Massacre in 1863, he agreed to settle the Shoshone people on the Fort Hall Indian Reservation.

Ezra Pound

Ezra Pound (1885–1972), who was born in Hailey, was among the greatest poets of the 20th century. He is best known for a long, incomplete poem called "The Cantos."

Edward Pulaski See page 63.

Thomas "Les" Purce (1946–) became the first African American to gain high elective office in Idaho when he was elected mayor of Pocatello in 1975. He went on to be an educator and university administrator.

Martha Raddatz (1953–), born in Idaho Falls, is a TV news reporter who appears on *World News with Diane Sawyer*, *Nightline*, and other shows. She is the author of the best seller *The Long Road Home: A Story of War and Family*, a book about the war in Iraq.

Marilynne Robinson (1943–) is an acclaimed novelist whose works include *Gilead* and *Housekeeping*. She grew up in Sandpoint.

Sacagawea See page 35.

J. R. Simplot See page 104.

Pocatello

Nikki Sixx (1958–) moved from California to Jerome, Idaho, where he learned to play bass guitar. In 1980, he founded the band Mötley Crüe with drummer Tommy Lee. To date, the band has sold more than 80 million albums.

Allen Slickpoo (1929–2013) grew up on the Nez Perce reservation in northern Idaho. He preserved his people's history in *Nu Mee Poom Tit Wah Tit: Nez Perce Legends*.

Robert Smylie (1914–2004) served as governor of Idaho from 1955 to 1967. He improved education and health care in the state and expanded the state park system.

Eliza Hart Spalding (1807–1851) was a Christian missionary in Idaho and Oregon.

Henry Harmon Spalding (1803–1874) was a missionary who, with his wife, Eliza Hart Spalding, established a mission among the Nez Perce people at Lapwai. He brought the first printing press to the Pacific Northwest.

Frank Steunenberg (1861–1905) was governor of Idaho from 1897 to 1901. He declared martial law during the Coeur d'Alene mine strike of 1899 and was assassinated in 1905 by Albert Horsley.

Picabo Street See page 87.

Dennis Sullivan (1942–) of Cottonwood is a sculptor who creates wooden statues of dogs.

Wallace Thurman (1902–1934) was a novelist and editor during the Harlem Renaissance, a flowering of African American art and literature in New York City in the 1920s and 1930s. He grew up in Boise.

Ted Trueblood (1913–1982), born in Boise, was an environmentalist and a writer for outdoor magazines. In 1936, he helped organize the Idaho Wildlife Federation, which fought to protect the state's natural beauty and wildlife.

Lana Turner

Lana Turner (1921–1995) was a glamorous film actor who appeared in films such as *Imitation of Life* and *The Bad and the Beautiful*. She was born in Wallace.

Darwin K. Vest See page 19.

Dawn Wells (1938–) played Mary Ann Summers on the long-running TV series *Gilligan's Island*. She lives part-time in Driggs, where she started the Idaho Film and Television Institute.

Benedicte Wrensted (1859–1949) was a Danish-born photographer who settled in Pocatello in 1895. The Smithsonian Institution in Washington, D.C., has collected her photos of American Indians and white settlers in the Pocatello area.

Nathaniel Wyeth See page 40.

Dawn Wells

RESOURCES

★ ★ ★

BOOKS

Nonfiction

Bolen, Robert David. *American Indian Tribes of Idaho*. Nampa, Idaho: Fort Boise Publishing Company, 2009.

Davenport, John. *The Internment of Japanese Americans During World War II*. New York: Chelsea House, 2010.

Dwyer, Helen, and Mary A. Stout. *Nez Perce History and Culture*. New York: Gareth Stevens Publishing, 2012.

Gondosch, Linda. *Where Did Sacagawea Join the Corps of Discovery? And Other Questions About the Lewis and Clark Expedition*. Minneapolis, Minn.: Lerner, 2011.

Hopping, Lorraine Jean. *Chief Joseph: The Voice for Peace*. New York: Sterling, 2010.

Sanford, William R. *John C. Frémont: Courageous Pathfinder of the Wild West*. Berkeley Heights, N.J.: Enslow Publishers, 2013.

Stanley, John. *Idaho: Past and Present*. New York: Rosen Central, 2010.

Fiction

Balch, Glenn. *Buck, Wild*. New York: Crowell, 1976.

Creech, Sharon. *Walk Two Moons*. New York: Joanna Cotler Books, 1995.

Crutcher, Chris. *The Sledding Hill*. New York: Harper Tempest, 2006.

Farrell, Mary Cronk. *Fire in the Hole!* New York: Clarion Books, 2004.

George, Jean Craighead. *Fire Storm*. New York: Katherine Tegen, 2003.

Ingold, Jeanette. *The Big Burn*. San Diego: Harcourt Brace, 2002.

FACTS FOR NOW

Visit this Scholastic Web site for more information on Idaho:
www.factsfornow.scholastic.com
Enter the keyword **Idaho**

INDEX

★ ★ ★

AUTHOR'S TIPS AND SOURCE NOTES

★ ★ ★

Several books on Idaho proved valuable in my research. Among them were *In Mountain Shadows: A History of Idaho* by Carlos A. Schwantes; *Idaho Echoes in Time: Traveling Idaho's History and Geology* by R. G. Robertson; and *Idaho: A Bicentennial History* by F. Ross Peterson.

Cort Conley and his colleagues at the Idaho Commission on the Arts were a wonderful resource, searching out information on Idaho artists. I'd like to extend my special thanks to Allen Slickpoo Jr. for granting me a personal interview about the Nez Perce people and his father's life and work.